PSYCHOLOGY OF PUNISHMENT

NEW RESEARCH

PSYCHOLOGY OF EMOTIONS, MOTIVATIONS AND ACTIONS

Additional books in this series can be found on Nova's website under the Series tab.

Additional e-books in this series can be found on Nova's website under the e-book tab.

PSYCHOLOGY OF EMOTIONS, MOTIVATIONS AND ACTIONS

PSYCHOLOGY OF PUNISHMENT

NEW RESEARCH

NICOLAS CASTRO
EDITOR

nova publishers
New York

Library of Congress Cataloging-in-Publication Data

Psychology of punishment : new research / editor, Nicolas Castro.
　　pages cm
　Includes index.
　ISBN: 978-1-62948-103-6 (hardcover)
　1. Punishment (Psychology) 2. Punishment. I. Castro, Nicolas.
　BF319.5.P8P7933 2013
　303.3'6--dc23
                            2013034688

Published by Nova Science Publishers, Inc. † New York

CONTENTS

PREFACE

In this book, the authors present current research on the study of the psychology of punishment. Topics discussed in this compilation include effective punishment experiences and the need for a more comprehensive approach to conceptualizing behavioral punishers and reinforcers in a road safety context; differences in the process of choosing capital punishment or imprisonment and excerpts from a study by a Japanese lay judge; punishment avoidance and intentional risky driving behaviors; an overview of delayed punishment and future directions; corporal physical punishment today; and the role of gender and school type in EFL teachers' adoption of classroom discipline strategies.

Chapter 1 – Determining what consequences are likely to serve as effective punishment for any given behaviour is a complex task. This chapter focuses specifically on illegal road user behaviours and the mechanisms used to punish and deter them. Traffic law enforcement has traditionally used the threat and/or receipt of legal sanctions and penalties to deter illegal and risky behaviours. This process represents the use of positive punishment, one of the key behaviour modification mechanisms. Behaviour modification principles describe four types of reinforcers: positive and negative punishments and positive and negative reinforcements. The terms 'positive' and 'negative' are not used in an evaluative sense here. Rather, they represent the presence (positive) or absence (negative) of stimuli to promote behaviour change. Punishments aim to inhibit behaviour and reinforcements aim to encourage it. This chapter describes a variety of punishments and reinforcements that have been and could be used to modify illegal road user behaviours. In doing so, it draws on several theoretical perspectives that have defined behavioural reinforcement and punishment in different ways. Historically, the main theoretical approach used to deter risky road use has been classical deterrence theory which has focussed on the perceived certainty, severity and swiftness of penalties. Stafford and Warr (1993) extended the traditional deterrence principles to include the positive reinforcement concept of punishment avoidance. Evidence of the association between punishment avoidance experiences and behaviour has been established for a number of risky road user behaviours including drink driving, unlicensed driving, and speeding. The authors chose a novel way of assessing punishment avoidance by specifying two sub-constructs (detection evasion and punishment evasion). Another theorist, Akers, described the idea of competing reinforcers, termed differential reinforcement, within social learning theory (1977). Differential reinforcement describes a balance of reinforcements and punishments as influential on behaviour. This chapter describes comprehensive way of conceptualising a broad range of reinforcement and punishment concepts, consistent with Akers' differential reinforcement concept, within a behaviour modification framework that incorporates deterrence principles. The efficacy of three theoretical perspectives to explain self-reported speeding among a sample of 833 Australian car drivers was examined. Results demonstrated that a broad range of variables predicted speeding including personal experiences of evading detection and punishment for speeding, intrinsic sensations, practical benefits expected from speeding, and an absence of punishing effects from being caught. Not surprisingly, being younger was also significantly related to more frequent speeding, although in a regression analysis, gender did not retain a significant influence once all punishment and reinforcement variables were entered. The implications for speed management, as well as road user behaviour modification more generally, are discussed in light of these findings. Overall, the findings reported in this chapter suggest that a more comprehensive approach is required to manage the behaviour of road users which does not rely solely on traditional legal penalties and sanctions.

Chapter 2 – The purpose of this study is to clarify the difference between decision-making processes that result in capital punishment and other forms of punishment, as made by lay judges in Japan. In this study, 126 Japanese undergraduate students listened to an audio recording of a fictitious murder trial and were asked to determine a punishment for the defendant ranging from several years' imprisonment to the death penalty. They were then split into two groups according to whether they chose the death penalty or not. This was followed by a comprehensive comparison of the verdicts of the two groups covering every angle. The results show that members of the group that chose the death penalty were already in favor of it before the study, and that the group that chose the death penalty evaluated the arguments and mitigating evidence in the trial in a disadvantageous way for the defendant. Finally, the most significant finding was that the group favoring the death penalty cited deterrence and retribution as reasons for their decision, while the group favoring imprisonment cited rehabilitation and retribution. A majority of earlier studies have shown that ordinary citizens do not consider deterrence and retribution together when determining punishment, while awarding the death penalty involves the consideration of both, which causes stress and anxiety for the lay judge. This study demonstrates that, in order to free themselves of this burden, lay judges likely justify death penalty decisions by reminding themselves that it deters crime in addition to its retributive purpose.

Chapter 3 – Every motorised jurisdiction mandates legal driving behaviour which facilitates driver mobility and road user safety through explicit road rules that are enforced by regulatory authorities such as the Police. In road safety, traffic law enforcement has been very successfully applied to modify road user behaviour, and increasingly technology is fundamental in detecting illegal road user behaviour. Furthermore, there is also sound evidence that highly visible and/or intensive enforcement programs achieve long-term deterrent effects. To illustrate, in Australia random breath testing has considerably reduced the incidence and prevalence of driving whilst under the influence of alcohol. There is, however, evidence that many road rules continue to be broken, including speeding and using a mobile phone whilst driving, and there are many instances where drivers are not detected or sufficiently sanctioned for these transgressions. Furthermore, there is a growing body of evidence suggesting that experiences of punishment avoidance – that is, successful attempts at avoiding punishment such as drivers talking themselves out of a ticket, or changing driving routes to evade detection –are associated with and predictive of the extent of illegal driving behaviour and future illegal driving intentions. Therefore there is a need to better understand the phenomenon of punishment avoidance to enhance our traffic law enforcement procedures and therefore safety of all road users. This chapter begins with a review of the young driver road safety problem, followed by an examination of contemporary deterrence theory to enhance our understanding of both the experiences and implications of punishment avoidance in the road environment. It is noteworthy that in situations where detection and punishment remain relatively rare, such as on extensive road networks, the research evidence suggests that experiences of punishment avoidance may have a stronger influence upon risky driving behaviour than experiences of punishment. Finally, data from a case study examining the risky behaviour of young drivers will be presented, and the implications for 'getting away with it' will be discussed.

Chapter 4 – Years of research on the effective use of punishers has shown that the most effective punishers are those which a) are intense, b) are inescapable, c) occur after every response, d) do not compete against reinforcers, e) are removed and then reintroduced, and f) are delivered immediately following a response. Although these qualities have been shown to increase a punisher's effectiveness, they are often difficult to control outside of laboratory settings. From a clinical perspective, one of the most difficult qualities to control may be the immediate delivery of a punisher, and for a variety of reasons there may be a delay between a response and the delivery of a scheduled punisher. Despite this reality, little recent research has been conducted on strategies to increase the suppressive effect of a delayed punisher. In this chapter we will describe the delay-of-punishment gradient (Kamin, 1959) as well as discuss the implications for the clinical application of punishers. We will review both basic and applied research on the effective use of delayed punishers and highlight applied studies demonstrating behavior suppression with delayed punishers. Finally, the authors will discuss the importance of conducting further research focused on increasing the suppressive effect of a delayed punisher.

Chapter 5 – Physical punishment, an ancient practice, has been the locus of recent discussion, research, and legislation. This chapter will explore corporal punishment in the United States, and review research that addresses the practices' effect on short and long term mental health. In addition to discussing discrepant prevalence rates and professional and public opinions, this chapter will address the connection between physical punishment and clinically diagnosable disorders, and other related mental health and well-being factors. Recommendations will be made regarding how to educate parents and encourage effective behavioral management, with a special emphasis on noting important risk and protective factors for the detrimental effects of corporal punishment on youth. Finally, the United States' hesitance to legislate against corporal punishment will be explored, and the negative effects of its proliferation will be discussed.

Chapter 6 – The aim of the current study was investigating the role of gender and school type (private and public) in EFL teachers' adoption of discipline strategies from their students' perspective. One thousand and four hundred eight students expressed their perceptions of the strategies their English teachers used to discipline the class on five main factors including punishment, recognition/reward, discussion, involvement/hinting, and aggression. The findings revealed that male and female teachers' adoption of discipline strategies was significantly different and female teachers were perceived to use punitive (punishment and aggression) and discussion strategies more frequently than male teachers. Further, it was found that public and private school teachers were different with respect to the strategies they implemented to discipline their classes. While public school teachers used aggression strategies more than private school teachers, private school teachers used discussion strategies more than public school teachers. The interaction of gender by school-type was also found to be statistically significant, implying that female teachers who worked in private schools tended to use involvement/hinting strategies more than other teachers while female teachers who worked in public schools were found to use punitive strategies more frequently in comparison to other teachers.

In: Psychology of Punishment
Editor: Nicolas Castro

ISBN: 978-1-62948-103-6
© 2013 Nova Science Publishers, Inc.

Chapter 1

EFFECTIVE PUNISHMENT EXPERIENCES: THE NEED FOR A MORE COMPREHENSIVE APPROACH TO CONCEPTUALISING BEHAVIOURAL PUNISHERS AND REINFORCERS IN A ROAD SAFETY CONTEXT

Judy Fleiter, Barry Watson and Alexia Lennon*
Centre for Accident Research and Road Safety-Queensland (CARRS-Q),
Queensland University of Technology

ABSTRACT

Determining what consequences are likely to serve as effective punishment for any given behaviour is a complex task. This chapter focuses specifically on illegal road user behaviours and the mechanisms used to punish and deter them. Traffic law enforcement has traditionally used the threat and/or receipt of legal sanctions and penalties to deter illegal and risky behaviours. This process represents the use of positive punishment, one of the key behaviour modification mechanisms. Behaviour modification principles describe four types of reinforcers: positive and negative punishments and positive and negative reinforcements. The terms 'positive' and 'negative' are not used in an evaluative sense here. Rather, they represent the presence (positive) or

---

* Corresponding author: j.fleiter@qut.edu.au.

absence (negative) of stimuli to promote behaviour change. Punishments aim to inhibit behaviour and reinforcements aim to encourage it. This chapter describes a variety of punishments and reinforcements that have been and could be used to modify illegal road user behaviours. In doing so, it draws on several theoretical perspectives that have defined behavioural reinforcement and punishment in different ways. Historically, the main theoretical approach used to deter risky road use has been classical deterrence theory which has focussed on the perceived certainty, severity and swiftness of penalties. Stafford and Warr (1993) extended the traditional deterrence principles to include the positive reinforcement concept of punishment avoidance. Evidence of the association between punishment avoidance experiences and behaviour has been established for a number of risky road user behaviours including drink driving, unlicensed driving, and speeding. We chose a novel way of assessing punishment avoidance by specifying two sub-constructs (detection evasion and punishment evasion). Another theorist, Akers, described the idea of competing reinforcers, termed differential reinforcement, within social learning theory (1977). Differential reinforcement describes a balance of reinforcements and punishments as influential on behaviour. This chapter describes comprehensive way of conceptualising a broad range of reinforcement and punishment concepts, consistent with Akers' differential reinforcement concept, within a behaviour modification framework that incorporates deterrence principles. The efficacy of three theoretical perspectives to explain self-reported speeding among a sample of 833 Australian car drivers was examined. Results demonstrated that a broad range of variables predicted speeding including personal experiences of evading detection and punishment for speeding, intrinsic sensations, practical benefits expected from speeding, and an absence of punishing effects from being caught. Not surprisingly, being younger was also significantly related to more frequent speeding, although in a regression analysis, gender did not retain a significant influence once all punishment and reinforcement variables were entered. The implications for speed management, as well as road user behaviour modification more generally, are discussed in light of these findings. Overall, the findings reported in this chapter suggest that a more comprehensive approach is required to manage the behaviour of road users which does not rely solely on traditional legal penalties and sanctions.

INTRODUCTION

There are many examples from around the world of countries that have experienced reductions in the number of road crashes and associated deaths and injuries over recent decades (World Health Organization, 2013). Improvements in road infrastructure and vehicle safety have played significant roles in these reductions. Improvements in road user behaviour (drivers, riders, pedestrians) have also played a part, with reductions in some high risk or illegal behaviours contributing to these successes. However, changing road user behaviour is not straightforward or easy and has, in many instances, taken long periods of time and considerable resources to produce the changes that many countries have experienced (Johnston, 2010; McLean, 2012).

A major mechanism that has driven road user behaviour change is effective and sustained traffic law enforcement, coupled with ongoing community awareness campaigns (Bates, Watson & Soole, 2012). This chapter will review research findings relating to enforcement-based approaches to road user behaviour change, drawing primarily on experiences from Australia. It does so through examining three theoretical perspectives that have been applied to the study of risky and illegal road use. It also describes limitations of the enforcement-based approach to behaviour change and discusses alternative mechanisms that could be harnessed, drawing upon behaviour modification concepts. Focussing specifically on the high risk behaviour of speeding, this chapter explores the reinforcing factors that influence driver speed choice among a sample of car drivers in Queensland, Australia.

Deterrence Theory

Historically, traffic law enforcement has used the threat of legal sanctions and penalties to deter illegal and risky behaviours which is based on classical deterrence principles. The traditional or classical form of deterrence theory is based on the Deterrence Doctrine which posits that individuals give rational consideration to their behavioural choices, based on the threat of associated sanctions (Gibbs, 1979). This threat is determined by a combination of the perceived risk of being apprehended and the perceived certainty, severity, and swiftness of punishments associated with apprehension (Homel, 1988; Vingilis, 1990). From this perspective, it is important that road users perceive that there is a chance they will be apprehended when committing an offence. Without this perception, the threat of punishment is likely to be rendered irrelevant (Kleck, Sever, Li & Gertz, 2005).

Advancements in technology have enhanced the opportunity to promote the concept of a high likelihood of apprehension for traffic offences (Bates et al., 2012). For instance, for those who exceed posted speed limits, automated speed enforcement has provided the potential for all offending motorists to be detected and to subsequently receive punishment. This situation is different to the levels of apprehension that are likely to be attained by on-road police patrols because the patrols occur only for a specific time, whereas fixed speed cameras operate around the clock (Shuey, 2004). Thus, the use of automated speed enforcement is one way that the perceived risk of apprehension can be raised among the motoring public. A similar increase in perceptions of the certainty of punishment once detected could be anticipated with the use of automated speed enforcement because determinations about speeding violations are made after the offence is committed and in a location that is totally removed from the roadside. In other words, the opportunity for a motorist to attempt to persuade a patrolling police officer that there are circumstances which may negate the need to issue them with an offence notice is removed via automation of the determination process. However, while automated speed enforcement may increase perceptions about apprehension and punishment certainty, receiving an offence notice several weeks after committing the offence, via the automated process, is not likely to increase perceptions about the swiftness of the punishment. This particular deterrence concept, swiftness of punishment, has received the least empirical support in the broader deterrence literature and it remains unclear exactly how relevant this aspect is for modifying road user behaviour (Nagin & Pogarsky, 2001).

Despite the intuitive logic of the principles of deterrence, empirical support has been mixed (Davey & Freeman, 2011; Ross, 1982). Gibbs (1979) provided a number of explanations for this outcome including the original unsystematic nature of deterrence as a doctrine, rather than a comprehensive theoretical explanation of behaviour, the complexity of issues obtained in the doctrine, and the difference between the objective and perceptual properties of punishment. Objective properties refer to actual punishments administered by the law whereas perceptual properties refer to an individual's perception of such. With respect to severity of punishment, for example, the actual penalty for committing an offence may be perceived as very severe by some drivers and not at all severe by others. In this way, the perceptual properties take on greater import than do actual legislated sanctions.

Furthermore, research has indicated that greater perceived certainty and severity of punishments do not always have the desired deterrent effect, but may, at least for some motorists, actually serve to reinforce illegal behaviour. For instance, Piquero and Paternoster (1998) found that drivers who had been punished for drink driving appeared more likely to re-offend and, counter intuitively, reported a lower perception of punishment certainty than those who had not been punished. Similar results were found when university students in the USA were asked to consider a scenario that would likely lead them to drive home after consuming enough alcohol to render them above the legal blood alcohol limit (Piquero & Pogarsky, 2002). There were significant correlations between those who had previously experienced punishment for this offence and perceptions of punishment certainty – those who had already been punished reported greater perceptions of punishment certainty. Results similar to this have also been found in relation to speeding.

For example, research conducted over several years in Queensland, Australia, examined the frequency with which drivers reported exceeding speed limits and found that greater certainty of punishment was not necessarily a deterrent to speeding. Results indicated that the more certain a driver was of being punished for speeding, the more frequently he/she reported engaging in speeding (Fleiter & Watson, 2006; Fleiter, Watson, Lennon, King & Shi, 2009). Pogarsky and Piquero (2003) have suggested that the selection hypothesis may account for this anomaly, where those apprehended more often are exposed to more direct punishment and are, therefore, more likely to perceive that punishment is highly likely (i.e., certain) when caught again, compared to those who do not offend or have not yet been caught. In this sense, punishment occurs in conjunction with an offence, yet may not necessarily discourage future offending. Piquero and Pogarsky (2002) have also used the term 'an emboldening effect' to describe this situation to explain why previous punishment experiences may be ineffective in deterring some people from reoffending.

Similarly, empirical results regarding punishment severity have not always been consistent with deterrence-based hypotheses. Theoretically, the perception that punishment will be severe should discourage offending. However, the doubling of speeding penalties in Sweden in the early 1980s did not lead to a decrease in speeding in a covert operation measuring speeds of over 40,000 vehicles. Furthermore, increases in fines five years later still did not result in changes to speeding (Andersson, 1989, as cited in Fildes & Lee, 1993). Similarly, research investigating increases in speeding penalties in 2003 in Queensland, Australia, found limited evidence of reductions in offending among drivers already convicted of speeding, particularly amongst repeat offenders (Watson, Siskind, Fleiter & Watson, 2010). More specifically, when investigating the offence history of those who went on to re-offend, the new, more severe penalties appeared to have little positive impact on repeat speeders because, contrary to predictions, there was a significant reduction in the length of time to re-offence and no significant change in the average number of offences they committed.

A similar pattern of results has been found in regard to drink driving. In the Australian state of New South Wales, no significant deterrent effect of higher penalties was found among all drink driving offenders dealt with by local courts between 2003 and 2004 (Weatherburn & Moffatt, 2011). Furthermore, in a study examining sanction perceptions of 166 drink driving recidivists in Queensland, the majority of offenders (86%) reported the belief that the sanctions associated with their conviction were severe, yet sanction severity was not a significant predictor of intentions to re-offend (Freeman et al., 2006). Similarly, a study in the USA compared perceptions of sanction severity with alcohol-related problems of 521 drink driving offenders (Yu, 2000). Sanction severity was assessed using measures of whether jail sentences were received, the number of months of licence suspension, licence withdrawal and/or revocation, and the monetary fine imposed. Results indicated that the severity of penalties did not substantially reduce drink driving recidivism, when controlling for alcohol-related problems. The length of a jail sentence showed a significant effect only in relation to those who had been convicted on four occasions. When considered together, these findings from studies across a range of illegal road user behaviours indicate that the traditional deterrence principles have some limitations in explaining offending.

Extending Deterrence Concepts

Recognising conceptual limitations with the traditional form of deterrence theory, Stafford and Warr (1993) examined the influence of previous punishment experiences in shaping behaviour. They proposed that the experience of committing an offence, but avoiding punishment for it, could exert a powerful influence on behaviour. Indeed they suggested that experiences of avoiding punishment may be a stronger reinforcer than actual punishment, particularly in circumstances where detection and punishment are relatively rare. The two concepts of punishment and punishment avoidance are central to the expanded version of deterrence theory. Further, they are described from the perspectives of self (personal/or direct experiences) and other people (vicarious/indirect experiences). This reconceptualised version has been applied to various road user behaviours and has shown consistent results regarding the strength of punishment avoidance in reinforcing behaviour.

For instance, among a sample of university students in Queensland, vicarious and personal punishment avoidance experiences, compared to other factors including perceptions of social rewards, attitudes and personality factors, were most strongly associated with self-reported drug driving (Armstrong, Wills & Watson, 2005). Another examination of drug driving in Queensland among a mixed sample (university students and drug referral program participants) found that the influence of punishment avoidance experiences differed according to gender (Watling, Freeman, Palk & Davey, 2011). For males, vicarious punishment avoidance experiences were found to be a more influential predictor of future intentions to drug drive than were experiences of personal punishment avoidance. However, the opposite result was found for female participants; personal experiences of avoiding punishment were more salient.

In the aforementioned investigation of speeding among Queensland drivers, findings indicated the significant influence of personal (direct) punishment avoidance on speeding with more avoidant experiences being a predictor of more frequent speeding (Fleiter & Watson, 2006). Personal and vicarious punishment experiences and vicarious punishment avoidance experiences were not significant predictors in that instance. Similar patterns of results have been found for both unlicensed driving and drink driving. Among a sample of 309 convicted unlicensed Queensland drivers, the experience of having avoided punishment when driving without a valid licence (defined as having come into contact with authorities but not having been asked to show their licence) was a significant predictor of more frequent unlicensed driving prior to detection, as well as greater intentions to drive unlicensed in future (Watson, 2004). Vicarious punishment avoidance experiences were not found to be a significant predictor, nor were personal or vicarious punishment experiences.

In results presented in another chapter of this book, almost one-sixth of a sample of 1,268 young novice drivers in Australia reported to have deliberately avoiding on-road police presence so as to avoid detection and subsequent punishment. These 'deliberate avoiders' were found to be more risky drivers across a range of measures and also anticipated engaging in riskier driving behaviour in future (Scott-Parker, Watson, King & Hyde, in press). This study appears to be the only one to have conceptualised punishment avoidance in terms of actual attempts to evade being detected for wrong doing. This issue of evading detection, as opposed to evading punishment once detected, is, we believe, an important distinction and is discussed in greater detail in the next section of this chapter.

Finally, in regard to drink driving, punishment avoidance experiences have been shown to be relevant in both an offender and a university student sample. Freeman & Watson (2006) found that repeat drink driving offenders' previous direct (but not vicarious) punishment avoidance experiences exerted the greatest influence on self-reported past drink driving behaviour and on intentions to drink drive in future. The aforementioned study of university students in the USA presented participants with a scenario about whether they would be likely to drive home after consuming enough alcohol to put them above the legal limit (Piquero & Pogarsky, 2002). Results indicated that previous personal and vicarious punishment and punishment avoidance experiences were predictive of the likelihood of driving home. Consistent with Stafford and Warr's extended deterrence model (1993), those with more personal experiences of having avoided punishment and knowing others who had done so were more likely to report that they would drive home. However, the finding that those with more personal and vicarious actual punishment experiences were also more likely to report that they would drive home when intoxicated is inconsistent with the revised deterrence theory, because punishment experiences are theorised as discouraging future offending.

Together, the findings from this body of research indicate that the additional concepts of punishment and punishment avoidance (both personal and vicarious) are useful concepts in better understanding the influence of penalties and sanctions on road users. However, they have not been able to account for all variance in behaviour. This presents a real challenge for those seeking to modify illegal driving behaviours, particularly via the traditional traffic law enforcement mechanisms that are based on deterrence principles. It also highlights that there is room to consider different approaches to modifying behaviour, including non-punitive methods. One theoretical perspective that offers an opportunity to consider a broader range of behavioural reinforcers is Akers' social learning theory (Akers, 1977), as discussed in the next section.

Social Learning Theory

Akers (1977) devised a version of social learning theory that combines sociological and psychological principles. It is a blend of differential association concepts as espoused by Sutherland (1947) (deviant behaviour occurs because of the presence of an excess of attitudes favourable towards law breaking over unfavourable ones, primarily gained from close associates), and the concepts of operant conditioning (differential reinforcement through reward and punishment) espoused by Skinner (1953) and vicarious learning (by imitating others) espoused by Bandura (1977). There are four main theoretical concepts in social learning theory: definitions (attitudes towards and rationalisations for behaviour), differential association (exposure to behaviour and definitions of others), imitation (modelling behaviours based on observing others) and differential reinforcement (the balance of actual and anticipated rewards and punishments associated with performing a behaviour). It is this fourth concept, differential reinforcement, which is most relevant to this chapter.

Differential reinforcement can be viewed from the perspective of a person weighing up the positive and negative aspects associated with performing a given behaviour. It proposes that previously rewarded behaviours increase the likelihood of repetition in the future, while previously punished behaviours will less likely be performed. Thus, according to social learning theory, it is the balance of these forces that determines behaviour as either conforming or deviant. Akers described differential reinforcement as encompassing: *a full range of behavioural inhibitors and facilitators: rewards/costs; past, present, and anticipated reinforcers and punishers; formal and informal sanctions; legal and extra-legal penalties; direct and indirect punishment; and positive and negative reinforcement* (Akers, 1990, p.655). Rewards and punishments are also described as being social and non-social in nature. Social reinforcements refer to immediate concrete interpersonal feedback from individuals and also to less tangible rewards, such as community support or disapproval. Non-social reinforcements, on the other hand, describe the effects of internal physiological and emotional arousal. This broad description of influences makes social learning theory ideal for studying the broad range of factors associated with risky road use. Moreover, it offers a mechanism for examining deterrence variables within differential reinforcement. The next section of this chapter describes how the various facets of Akers' differential reinforcement concept align with behaviour modification principles.

Behaviour Modification Principles within a Social Learning Context

Behaviour modification principles are based on the work of B.F Skinner (1953) and describe four types of reinforcers: positive and negative punishments and positive and negative reinforcements. The terms 'positive' and 'negative' are not used in an evaluative sense. Rather, they indicate the presence or absence of stimuli. The two punishment components inhibit behaviour while the two reinforcement components encourage it. The two positive components involve the presence of stimuli to alter behaviour, while the two negative components involve the removal of stimuli.

As noted above, the differential reinforcement concept within social learning theory was developed with the aim of encompassing a wide variety of rewarding and punishing experiences, including those outlined in the classic and extended forms of deterrence. To illustrate this proposition, Table 1 represents a consolidated approach to conceptualising these stimuli using the example of speeding, a high risk driver behaviour. This approach to conceptualising a broad range of reinforcers and punishers offers a comprehensive way of studying all the factors that may influence driving speeds. As can be seen in Table 1, the concept of punishment avoidance can be viewed in two ways. Extending upon the concept of simply avoiding punishment, as described by Stafford and Warr (1993), we have considered 'avoidance' in two ways: 1) evading detection when speeding, and 2) evading punishment if detected for speeding. In this way, avoidance can be viewed as a more comprehensive variable than simply evading legal sanctions if caught. Given that exceeding the speed limit is, by nature, a relatively common driver behaviour, even if inadvertently and by small amounts (Fleiter, Lennon & Watson, 2007; Ipsos Social Research Institute, 2013), we believe that the distinction between evading detection and evading penalties/sanctions is an important one, since they represent different means by which punishment is avoided.

Applications of Social Learning Theory to Explain Road User Behaviour

Although widely applied to a range of deviant behaviours (see Akers, 2009), Akers' social learning theory has had relatively little application to road user behaviour. Previous theoretical applications have offered support for the importance of differential reinforcement across a variety of road user behaviours. For instance, greater self-reported risky driving among young Queensland drivers was associated with greater anticipated rewards and fewer anticipated punishments, as well as imitating the risky driving of significant others (imitation) (Scott-Parker, Watson & King, 2009). In regard to unlicensed driving, social learning variables, notably anticipated punishments, were influential on self-reported intentions to drive unlicensed in the future and on the frequency of current unlicensed driving. In both instances, fewer anticipated punishments predicted greater intentions and greater current unlicensed driving (Watson, 2004). With regard to speeding, all social learning variables were found to significantly contribute to predicting self-reported speeding among a sample of Queensland drivers, with punishments (anticipated and actual) and rewards (anticipated and actual) found to be consistent with theoretical prediction, but not as strongly associated as imitation and definitions. Overall, this suggests that differential reinforcement concepts are important in influencing various road user behaviours, with anticipated or experienced punishments playing a key role.

Study Hypotheses

This study aimed to examine the efficacy of a range of reinforcement concepts to predict self-reported speeding. Based on previous research, we sought to examine how well the traditional deterrence-related concepts perform in predicting speeding, as well as examining any unique contribution of broader reinforcement concepts. Thus, the following hypotheses were derived:

1. The extended deterrence-based concepts will predict a greater proportion of variance in self-reported speeding than the traditional deterrence concepts alone;
2. The additional reinforcement concepts encompassed within social learning theory will predict a greater proportion of variance in self-reported speeding compared to the deterrence-based concepts.

METHOD

Participants

A total of 838 people participated in this study but only 833 questionnaires were used for analyses due to large amounts of missing data in 5 cases. Participants ranged in age from 17-85 years (Mean = 40.49 years, SD = 16.62) and just over one half of the sample (55.4%) were men. The vast majority of the sample held an Open (unrestricted) drivers licence from an Australian jurisdiction. International licence holders were excluded because it was not known to what extent they had been exposed to previous traffic enforcement activities in Australia.

Materials

A questionnaire containing a range of items and scales was created for the study, drawing on existing deterrence and social learning literature. While the questionnaire contained items assessing all four social learning variables, this chapter focuses specifically on the reinforcement constructs contained within social learning theory. The dependent variable, frequency of speeding, was selected as a general measure of current behaviour (i.e., self-reported speeding in the month immediately prior to participation). Measurement was based on an item used in the national road safety survey in Australia (Pennay, 2009) where participants were asked to nominate how frequently they had exceeded speed limits on urban (60 km/hr) and open roads (100 km/hr) by the following three amounts: *Less than 10km/hr, 10-20 km/hr,* and *More than 20 km/hr.* The Frequency of speeding variable was created by summing responses for each amount across both speed zones. The decision to combine the responses for both speed zones was based on the desire to characterise the network-wide speeding of participants in a holistic manner. Scores could range from 6 to 36 and higher scores reflect reports of exceeding the speed limit more often (i.e., more frequent speeding).

The independent variables were assessed as follows. Consistent with the broad range of influencers described by Akers, differential reinforcement was assessed using items and scales categorised as rewards and punishments described in Table 1. Unless otherwise stated, all items were scored using a 7 point Likert scale (1 = *Strongly disagree* to 7 = *Strongly agree*). Rewards were classified into three categories: social, instrumental, and non-social. Social rewards refer to actual or anticipated positive social feedback from others for speeding and were assessed by 3 items (e.g., *I get respect from my family members for exceeding the speed limit*). Instrumental rewards refer to the more practical outcomes associated with speeding and were assessed by 4 items (e.g., *I can save time by driving above the speed limit*). Non-social rewards refer to the positive intrinsic feelings associated with speeding. Seven items, including the four speeding-specific items of the Thrill Seeking Scale (Matthews, Desmond, Joyner, Carcary & Gilliland, 1996) were used (e.g., *I enjoy the sensation of accelerating rapidly*).

Table 1. Behaviour modification principles applied to speeding

	Reinforcements	Punishments
Positive	**Positive reinforcement** (REWARDS) *Stimuli occur and encourage speeding* **Social rewards** - *praise for speeding* **Instrumental rewards** - *save time by speeding* **Non-social rewards** - *excitement from speeding*	**Positive punishment** (PUNISHMENTS) *Stimuli occur and inhibit speeding* **Formal (personal, direct) social punishments** - *speeding tickets* **Informal social punishments** *–criticism from peers for speeding* **Non-social punishments** - *fear induced by speeding* **Vicarious punishment** - *knowledge of others receiving speeding tickets*
Negative	**Negative reinforcement** (LACK OF PUNISHMENT) *Stimuli are removed and encourage speeding* **Personal punishment avoidance** -*my experiences of evading detection when speeding and evading legal sanctions if caught speeding* **Vicarious punishment avoidance** - *others experiences of evading detection when speeding and evading legal sanctions if caught speeding* **Absence of punishing effect** - *receipt of sanctions means nothing to me*	**Negative punishment** (LACK OF REWARD) *Stimuli are removed and inhibit speeding* **Illusionary reward** – *failure to attain expected rewards from speeding (e.g., failure to receive expected praise from peers when speeding)*

Consistent with the concept of lack of punishment as a negative reinforcement, five scales were created. Two scales assessed personal experiences of evading detection (3 items, e.g., *How often have you avoided detection when speeding by: remaining watchful for police?, slowing down where you have seen speed cameras?*) and personal experiences of evading legal punishments (2 items; e.g., *How often have you evaded penalties for speeding by getting another person to say they were driving at the time of the offence?*) (scored 1=*Never* to 6=*Always*). Vicarious detection evasion and vicarious punishment evasion were also assessed using two scales that measured participants' knowledge of others who had evaded detection (3 items) and evaded punishment previously (2 items) (scored 1=*None* to 5=*All*). Finally, three items assessed the concept of absence of a punishing effect from formal sanctions (e.g., *If I got fined for speeding today, it would make no difference in my life*).

Punishments were operationalised to cover only the 'positive' aspects as depicted in the upper right-hand quadrant of Table 1. Social punishments were assessed various ways. Informal social punishments were assessed using four items examining expected reactions from significant others to the participant receiving a speeding ticket (e.g., *Suppose you got a speeding ticket yesterday...my friends would think it was silly of me to be driving faster than the speed limit*). Formal social punishments were assessed by asking participants to report the number of speeding tickets received in the previous three years. Non-social punishments were assessed using 4 items to assess negative intrinsic emotions/sensations associated with speeding (e.g., *I feel guilty if I drive above the speed limit*). Vicarious punishment was assessed by asking participants to nominate the number of people they were aware of who had received a speeding ticket in the previous three years. As noted above, only positive punishments were assessed. Negative punishments (lack of reward) was not operationalised in this study because in qualitative research examining factors influential to speeding, this construct was not found to be a salient influence.

The traditional deterrence-related variables (i.e., perceived risk of apprehension and the perceived certainty, severity and swiftness of punishment) can be considered as additional ways of measuring direct punishment experiences. Perceived risk of apprehension when speeding was assessed by asking participants how likely they thought it was that they would be caught if they were driving more than 10 km/hr above the posted limit on an open road (scored 1=*Extremely unlikely* to 7=*Extremely likely*). This wording was chosen to reflect previous qualitative findings where some drivers described the belief that travel speeds of less than 10 km/hr above the posted limit were not considered as speeding (Fleiter et al., 2007). Perceived certainty of punishment was assessed by asking participants how likely it was that they would be fined and lose demerit points if caught speeding (scored 1=*Extremely unlikely* to 7=*Extremely likely*). Perceived severity of punishment was assessed by asking participants to nominate how harsh they thought the fines and demerit point penalties for speeding were (scored 1=*Not at all severe* to 5=*Very severe*). Finally, perceived swiftness of penalty was assessed by asking participants to report whether they believed that there was a short delay between getting caught for speeding and receiving the legal penalties.

Procedure

Participants were recruited from vehicle service stations at three regional locations adjacent to the major north-south highway in Queensland, Australia. These locations are situated approximately 35, 290, and 650 kilometres north of the capital city and represent metropolitan and regional areas. In each location, venues on both sides of the road were selected to ensure there was no systematic bias introduced from sampling unidirectional traffic flow. In addition, three fuel companies (2 major and 1 independent) were selected in an attempt to increase sample representativeness. Customers in the restaurant areas of venues were approached, once seated at a table, and asked to voluntarily participate in a survey on driving experiences. On average, questionnaires took 25-30 minutes to complete. Participants were offered AUD10 cash upon completion of the questionnaire. A response rate of 29.09% was attained.

RESULTS

Descriptive Statistics

Means, standard deviations, score ranges and reliability co-efficients (Cronbach's alpha) for the independent variables are presented in Table 2. All scales demonstrated moderate to very high internal reliability (Cronbach's alphas ranging from .70 to .93).

In regard to the Reinforcements variables, from the information presented in Table 2, it can be seen that the mean score for Social rewards was low (4.98), indicating that overall, positive feedback for speeding from important others was not commonly reported. Similarly, a relatively low mean score for Instrumental rewards (13.11) indicates that the sample did not strongly endorse the practical outcomes associated with speeding (e.g., saving time). For non-social rewards, the low mean score suggests that for this sample, thrill seeking tendencies relating to speeding were low overall.

In relation to direct avoidance experiences, the mean scores indicate that participants admitted personally evading detection for speeding much more commonly than they did for evading legal punishments once detected. Given the illegal nature of the activities used as sample items for the punishment avoidance scale, this finding is not surprising. Conversely, the pattern of results for the two indirect avoidance scales was in the opposite direction. In regard to vicarious detection evasion and punishment evasion experiences, the mean scores in Table 2 demonstrate that participants endorsed responses indicating that they were aware of more people who used illegal activities to evade punishment once detected than they were of people who employed strategies to evade detection when speeding. This finding might be explained by drivers only discussing with others the strategies they use to evade punishment (e.g., getting another licence holder to say they were driving at the time of the offence), rather than discussing more mundane strategies such as watching for other cars flashing their headlights to warn of enforcement ahead. The mean score of 7.53 for the scale that assess the absence of a punishing effect from penalties was well below the scale mid-point. This indicates that overall, participants generally disagreed with the notion that being apprehended and receiving the associated legal penalties did not produce a punishing effect.

Table 2. Descriptive statistics for Reinforcements and Punishments (independent variables)

Variable name	Mean	SD	Range	Reliability
REINFORCEMENTS				
Social rewards	4.98	3.2	3-21	.86
Instrumental rewards	13.11	6.6	5-35	.80
Non-social rewards	18.28	11.01	7-49	.91
Personal detection avoidance	8.53	4.43	3-18	.89
Personal punishment avoidance	2.25	1.03	2-12	.78
Vicarious detection avoidance	3.08	1.38	3-15	.93
Vicarious punishment avoidance	8.31	3.32	2-10	.92
Absence of punishing effect	7.53	4.33	3-21	.70
PUNISHMENTS				
Formal social (speeding tickets)*	0.57	1.24	0-20	-
Informal social punishment	20.8	6.8	4-28	.80
Non-social punishment	19.98	4.3	4-28	.76
Vicarious punishment*	3.64	4.83	0-23	-
Perceived risk of apprehension*	5.03	1.86	1-7	-
Perceived certainty of punishment	6.52	3.19	2-14	.93
Perceived severity of punishment	6.9	1.99	2-14	.83
Perceived swiftness of punishment*	4.59	1.81	1-7	-

* A reliability assessment was not applicable because these variables were not assessed as scales.

Turning to the Punishments variables, the mean number of speeding tickets (formal social punishments) reported as received in the previous three years was 0.57. Approximately one third of the sample (32.53%, n=271) reported having received at least one infringement. Of the 271 people who reported receiving a ticket, the majority (61.25%) reported only one ticket, and 6.3% reported having received four or more. Informal social punishments assessed anticipated negative reactions from friends and family to being apprehended for speeding. The mean score of 20.8 suggests that overall, participants agreed that they would receive negative feedback from significant others if they were caught speeding. One item in this scale assessed whether participants would be embarrassed to tell others if they were booked for speeding. Approximately half the sample (47.9%) reported agreement with this statement. Together, these results indicate a strong perception about receiving social disapproval from family and friends for speeding among this sample. The mean score recorded for Non-social punishments for speeding indicates general overall agreement that feelings such as guilt and anxiety were associated with speeding for this sample. Participants indicated that they were aware of an average of 3.64 others who had received tickets for speeding in the last three years (i.e., vicarious punishment).

Finally, with regard to the four classical deterrence variables, when travelling at speeds of more than 10km/hr above the posted speed limit on an open road, responses indicated that there was a relatively high perceived risk of being caught (mean score of 5.03). This finding may reflect the perception, reported elsewhere, that police only enforce speeding once it reaches a limit that equates to either 10 km or 10% above posted speed limits (i.e., that the police use a speed enforcement tolerance or threshold) (Fleiter et al., 2009). With regard to perceptions about the certainty of receiving legal punishments if caught, participants did not necessarily perceive penalties as automatic. Approximately one third of the sample endorsed the response options *Somewhat* to *Extremely unlikely* to receive a monetary fine (35.8%) and a demerit point sanction (37.6%) if caught. For the items assessing perceptions about the severity of speeding penalties, approximately 10% of the sample reported penalties as not at all severe. A similar proportion viewed monetary and demerit penalties for speeding as extremely severe. Mean responses to the individual items indicate that demerit point penalties ($M = 3.12$, $SD = 1.05$) were viewed as significantly more severe than monetary penalties ($M = 2.95$, $SD = 1.03$); $t(832) = 85.34$, $p < .001$. Overall, the mean score was below the scale mid-point, suggesting that in general, participants did not perceive penalties for speeding as severe. Finally, with regard to perceptions about how swiftly penalties are delivered after being detected, results indicated that just over half of the sample (54.1%) reported the perception that penalties are not delivered in a short timeframe. The dependent variable, frequency of speeding, was a composite measure of how frequently drivers reported exceeding posted speed limits on open and urban roads by less than 10 km/hour, 10-20 km/hour and more than 20km/hour. The mean score of 11.12 (SD = 4.61) is below the mid-point of the scale. Responses ranged from 6 to 34 (possible range of scores was 6 to 36). The mean score indicates that more than half the sample reported that they do not frequently exceed the limit on these roads (60 km/hour urban roads and 100 km/hour open roads).

Bivariate Analyses

Table 3 contains information about the bivariate relationships of all independent variables with frequency of speeding. All significant correlations are reported, however those below 0.2 should be considered relatively weak (Kline, 1998).

Table 3. Bivariate relationships between all independent variables and frequency of speeding

	Bivariate relationship with Frequency of Speeding
Social rewards	.23[*]
Instrumental rewards	.56[*]
Non-social rewards	.52[*]
Absence of punishing effect	.39[*]
Personal detection evasion	.51[*]
Personal punishment evasion	.27[*]
Vicarious detection evasion	.32[*]
Vicarious punishment evasion	.41[*]
Formal social punishment (speeding tickets)	.24[*]
Informal social punishment	-.31[*]
Non-social punishment	-.35[*]
Vicarious punishment	.17[*]
Perceived risk of apprehension	-.19[*]
Perceived certainty of punishment	.16[*]
Perceived severity of punishment	.23[*]
Perceived swiftness of punishment	.04

* $p<.001$

All relationships except the one with perceived swiftness of punishment were significant ($p<.001$). Moderate, positive and significant relationships were found for instrumental (.56) and non-social rewards (.52), personal detection evasion (.51), and vicarious punishment evasion (.41). These associations were all in the expected theoretical direction and indicate those who reported more frequent speeding also reported attaining more practical rewards from speeding (e.g., saving time), more thrill or excitement from speeding, greater experiences of having personally evaded detection when speeding, and knowing a larger number of other people who had evaded punishment when detected.

The remaining, weaker relationships that were in the expected theoretical direction were absence of punishing effect (.39), non-social punishments (-.35), vicarious detection evasion (.32), informal social punishments (-.31), personal punishment evasion (.27), and perceived risk of apprehension (-.19). These results indicate that more frequent speeding was reported by those who perceived fewer negative effects from being caught speeding, perceived or had experienced fewer negative internal feelings when speeding (e.g., fear), knew more people who have evaded detection when speeding, anticipated or experienced less negative feedback from others about speeding, had more experiences of evading punishments when caught speeding, and perceived that there is a lower risk of being caught when speeding.

The remaining significant, yet weak associations were not in the expected theoretical direction: formal social punishment (.24), perceived severity (.23), vicarious punishment experiences (.17), and certainty of punishment (.16). These results indicate that those who reported more frequent speeding had previously received a greater number of speeding tickets, perceived speeding penalties as more severe, reported knowing more people who had received speeding penalties when caught, and perceived punishment as certain once detected.

Multivariate Analysis

In order to examine the two study hypotheses, an hierarchical regression analysis was conducted. Variables were entered in successive steps according to theoretical relevance. The first step consisted of participant age and gender because of their well documented strong links to driving speeds (i.e., being younger and male is associated with more speeding) (McCartt, Mayhew, Braitman, Ferguson & Simpson, 2009; Palamara & Stevenson, 2003; Patil,

Shope, Raghunathan & Bingham, 2006). The second step contained the classical deterrence variables, the third contained the extended deterrence variables and the fourth step represented all remaining reinforcement and punishment variables. Table 4 provides details of the analysis.

The overall model was significant, $F(8,814)=40.14$, $p<.001$, and accounted for 45.8% of the total variance in frequency of speeding. Age and gender accounted for 18.6% of the variance, $F(2,830) = 95.98$, $p<.001$. The classical deterrence variables accounted for a significant, additional 5.2% of variance, R^2 Cha $=.052$, $F(4, 826) = 14.06$, $p<.001$. The extended deterrence variables accounted for a significant, additional 15.1% of variance in frequency of speeding, R^2 Cha $=.151$, $F(6, 820) = 33.92$, $p<.001$. The final block of remaining reinforcement and punishment variables added another significant 7.9% of variance, R^2 Cha $=.079$, $F(6, 814) = 20.33$, $p<.001$.

As can be seen from the information presented in Table 4, eight variables were significant predictors in the final model (presented in bold text). In order of decreasing association, these significant predictors were: personal detection evasion ($\beta=.193$, $sr^2=.02$), instrumental rewards ($\beta=.19$, $sr^2=.02$), absence of punishing effect ($\beta=.114$, $sr^2=.009$), age ($\beta= -.111$, $sr^2=.008$), non-social rewards ($\beta=.107$, $sr^2=.005$), non-social punishments ($\beta= -.094$, $sr^2=.007$), direct punishment evasion ($\beta=.078$, $sr^2=.005$), and formal social punishment ($\beta=.074$, $sr^2=.004$). These results indicate that those people who reported more frequent speeding were those who: experienced more occasions of evading detection when they sped, anticipated more tangible rewards from speeding, expected fewer negative outcomes from apprehension and punishments for speeding, were younger, experienced greater intrinsic feelings of thrill/excitement when speeding, experienced fewer feelings of guilt or fear when speeding, experienced evading legal sanctions when caught speeding, and received more speeding tickets. Direction of associations in the final model indicates that all variables except one (formal social punishments/speeding tickets) were consistent with theoretical prediction. The positive beta weight for this variable indicates that people reported speeding more frequently if they had received a greater number of speeding tickets in the previous three years. This suggests that receiving a ticket was not necessarily deterring speeding (i.e., the opposite of the intended effect of the sanction).

Variable	Step 1			Step 2			Step 3			Step 4		
	B	p	sr^2	B	p	sr^2	B	p	sr^2	B	p	sr^2
Step 1												
Age	-.387	<.001	.15	-.339	<.001	.11	-.196	<.001		-.111	<.001	.008
Gender	-.21	.001	.04	-.164	<.001	.03	-.094	<.001		-.005	.869	
Step 2 Classical deterrence												
Risk Apprn				-.146	<.001	.02	-.112	<.001	.012	-.046	.090	
Certainty				.088	.005	.007	.044	.126		.035	.194	
Severity				.15	<.001	.02	.078	.007	.005	.050	.066	
Swiftness				.063	.041		.016	.572		.011	.678	
Step 3 Extended deterrence												
#Tickets							.100	.001	.008	.074	.008	.004
Personal Detect Evn							.316	<.001	.06	.193	<.001	.02
Personal Pun Evn							.093	.002	.007	.078	.006	.005
Vic Detect Evn							.050	.13		.024	.435	
Vic Pun Evn							.055	.139		.053	.129	
Vicarious pun							.021	.486		.014	.617	
Step 4 Other reinforcers												
Social Rwd										-.013	.664	
Instrl Rwd										.190	<.001	.02
Nonsoc Rd										.107	.007	.005
Absence of pun effect										.114	<.001	.009
Social Pun										.015	.631	
Non-social Pun										-.094	.002	.007
Adj R^2	.186			.234			.382			.458		
ΔR^2	.188			.052			.151			.079		

CONCLUSION

This chapter extends previous applications and understandings of penalties and sanctions traditionally associated with speeding by seeking to incorporate a broader focus on punishers and reinforcers as conceptualised through behaviour modification principles. Furthermore, to our knowledge, it is the only study that has conceptualised the construct of punishment avoidance to include two discrete sub-constructs: detection evasion and punishment evasion once detected. Two hypotheses were tested which were based on deterrence concepts as well as concepts based on operant conditioning.

The first hypothesis tested the efficacy of the extended deterrence concepts (Stafford & Warr, 1993) in explaining self-reported speeding, beyond what could be predicted by the classical deterrence principles, and by participant age and gender. The first part of the hierarchical regression analysis provided support for this hypothesis in that an additional 15.1% of variance in frequency of speeding was explained by the extended deterrence variables, over and above that explained uniquely by classical deterrence concepts (5.2%) and age and gender alone (18.6%). The results also supported the second hypothesis. The addition of a block of predicator variables that are grounded in behaviour modification principles (and are consistent with social learning theory's description of reinforcement concepts) was able to predict an additional and significant 7.9% of variance in frequency of speeding.

It is recognised that a broad range of personal, social, legal, and environmental factors influence driving speeds. The results described here indicate that one personal factor in particular, age, remains an important factor, yet is one that is not able to be directly altered by enforcement or education. Younger drivers reported more frequent speeding; a finding consistent with a wealth of speeding and risky driving research (Fernandes, Job & Hatfield, 2004; Hatfield & Fernandes, 2009; Scott-Parker, Hyde, Watson & King, 2013). Additionally, greater anticipated sensations of thrill and excitement from speeding (non-social rewards) and fewer anticipated feelings of fear or anxiety (non-social punishments) were also significant predictors of more frequent speeding. These personality-related factors have traditionally been found to be strongly associated with younger people, including young drivers (Jonah, 1997; Jonah, Thiessen & Au-Yeung, 2001) and represent a major challenge in speed management and promoting safe road use in general. Changes to graduated driver licensing programs have attempted to address these challenges by introducing measures for novice drivers such as restricting access to high powered vehicles, restricting top driving speeds, and reducing exposure of novice drivers to high risk times of the day (late night/early morning) (Senserrick, 2009; Whelan, Scully & Newstead, 2009). In addition, media campaigns have focussed on young drivers in an attempt to counter thrill seeking tendencies by highlighting things such as the social unacceptability of risky driving and placing others at risk (Lewis, Watson, White, and Elliott, 2013; Watsford, 2008). Ongoing efforts are clearly needed in this area.

Another important outcome highlighted from the current study is the importance of the need to counter experiences of evading detection when speeding and evading punishments when detected. Detecting every instance of speeding is currently not possible, given the large road network, the high prevalence of speeding, and the limited capacity of speed enforcement resources (Ipsos Social Research Institute, 2013; McLean, 2012). However, the results of this study indicate the importance of trying to negate the effects of evading detection when speeding, since it was the variable with the strongest association with speeding. The deployment of new speed management technologies may assist in this regard. Approaches such as point-to-point speed enforcement (also known as average speed control) are potentially able to contribute here. This approach sees cameras placed at numerous locations along a route, thereby allowing speeds to be monitored along much larger parts of the road network than is possible via fixed or mobile speed cameras (Soole, Watson & Fleiter, 2013). Evading legal penalties once detected was also a significant predictor. A variety of strategies to avoid receiving penalties have been reported across a range of countries. Examples include getting others to say that they were driving at the time of the offence, negotiating with police officers to avoid a ticket or reduce the size of the penalty, arguing with police, fraudulent use of others' demerit points, continuing to drive when unlicensed, using 'important' others to persuade police to cancel an infringement (i.e., police corruption) (Durrani, Waseem, Bhatti, Razzak & Naseer, 2011; Fleiter et al., 2007; Fleiter, Watson, Lennon, King & Shi, 2011; Scott-Parker, et al., in press). These activities pose significant challenges to maintaining the integrity of the legal penalty system. It is recognised that, because of their illegal nature, it is not possible to quantify the extent of such practices. However, efforts to counteract the impact of these activities are clearly needed.

Perceptions of greater tangible rewards from speeding (e.g., saving time) were also significantly related to more frequent speeding. A study conducted in the Australian state of Victoria used in-vehicle intelligent speed adaptation (ISA) devices to record data about a range of risky behaviours, including speeding, and provided some encouraging results in relation to saving time (Regan et al., 2007). For commuting trips, mean speeds decreased when using ISA, yet this did not equate to any appreciable increase in trip time. Publicising such results may assist in countering the perception that speeding saves time (Lewis et al., 2013; Raftery, Kleoden, & Royals, 2013). Another key predictor variable in the current study was the absence of negative outcomes when caught speeding. This is likely to be linked to the finding that the receipt of a greater number of speeding tickets was also associated with greater self-reported speeding; a finding that is contrary to theoretical prediction, yet consistent with a growing body of literature, as discussed in the introductory section of this chapter. Having previously received a speeding ticket appears to be ineffective in deterring speeding among some drivers. As noted earlier, Piquero and Pogasky (2002), labelled this an 'emboldening' effect (as opposed to a punishing one) and noted that it is possible that *'punishment serves merely to identify the most committed offenders, who then, not surprisingly, report a greater inclination toward future offending'* (p.178). Stafford and Warr (1993) suggested that *'offenders whose experience is limited largely to avoiding punishment may come to believe that they are immune from punishment, even in the face of occasional evidence to the contrary'* (p. 125). We suggest that the link between punishment avoidance and previous speeding infringements is one that warrants further investigation because it is possible that tickets and associated legal penalties are not viewed as salient enough to change behaviour among some (persistent) speeding drivers.

Some limitations are inherent in research of this nature and should be considered when interpreting the findings. Reliance on self-report data is acknowledged as potentially biasing because of the possibility for socially desirable responding. However, the relatively high level of community acceptance of speeding suggests that participants would not perceive the need to alter their responses to appear more socially appropriate (Corbett, 2001; McLean, 2012). Additionally, the self-report method relies on accurate recall of information and is, therefore, open to inaccuracies because of potential under- and over-reporting (Lajunen & Summala, 2003). However, a range of studies have examined the relationship between objective measures of speeding and self-reported speeding, revealing relatively high consistency between the two measures (for example, see Hagland & Aberg, 2002). It is also acknowledged that the recruitment strategy may have introduced some bias in sampling. A convenience sample of drivers was recruited from three sites on a major highway. This may have precluded people who do not regularly drive on this type of road (i.e., high speed). However, comparisons between the sample and the population of Queensland drivers revealed no anomalies in key characteristics among the research sample. Furthermore, participation was not restricted to people who drove on this highway because passengers were eligible to participate if they were current licence holders.

It is also acknowledged that the concept of negative punishment, as described in the lower right-hand quadrant of Table 1, was not assessed in this study. The experience of losing something of value from speeding, such as failing to gain expected rewards (e.g., praise from peers) for speeding is theorised as inhibiting speeding according to behaviour modification principles. Arguably, current community acceptance of speeding in Australia suggests that progress in this area is slow. Encouragingly however, as recently summarised by McLean (2012), great progress has been witnessed in Australia in relation to changing community attitudes towards other risky behaviours such as drink driving and non-use of seatbelts. Therefore, efforts to alter perceptions about speeding should continue.

In conclusion, this chapter has provided insight into how punishers and reinforcers can assist us to better understand the key influencers on drivers and to rethink the traditional penalty-based approach to managing speeds. While legal penalties are acknowledged as an important part of speed management, conceptualising a wide range of punishers and reinforcers, both positive and negative, offers the opportunity for society to explore other avenues to promote speed limit compliance and safer road use overall.

The findings described in this chapter highlight important implications for how we understand and develop road safety countermeasures in future. A more comprehensive approach to managing speeding, as well as managing other illegal road user behaviours, is needed if we are to capitalise on harnessing the influence of the broad range of behavioural influences discussed in this chapter. Moreover, this more comprehensive approach to conceptualising punishers and reinforcers is also likely to be relevant to other areas of criminological research where punishment avoidance and/or anticipated social rewards may be relatively common (e.g., substance abuse, juvenile crime). Therefore, future research across a range of illegal/risky behaviours may benefit from disentangling and better understanding the influence of the various factors examined and discussed in this chapter.

REFERENCES

Akers, R. L. (1977). *Deviant behaviour: A social learning approach* (2nd ed.). Belmont, California: Wadsworth Publishing Company.

Akers, R. L. (1990). Rational choice, deterrence, and social learning theory in criminology: The path not taken. *The Journal of Criminal Law and Criminology, 81*, 653-676.

Akers, R. L. (2009). *Social Learning and Social Structure: A General Theory of Crime and Deviance* New Jersey: Transaction Publishers.

Armstrong, K., Wills, A. & Watson, B. (2005). Psychosocial influences on drug driving in young Australian drivers *Australasian Road Safety Research Policing Education Conference* Wellington, New Zealand.

Bandura, A. (1977). *Social learning theory.* Englewood Cliffs, N.J.: Prentice Hall.

Bates, L. J., Soole, D.W., & Watson, B. (2012) The effectiveness of traffic policing in reducing traffic crashes. In Prenzler, Tim (Ed.) *Policing and Security in Practice : Challenges and Achievements.* Palgrave Macmillan, United Kingdom.

Corbett, C. (2001). Explanations for "understanding" in self-reported speeding behaviour. *Transportation Research Part F, 4*, 133-150.

Davey, J. & Freeman, J. (2011). Improving road safety through deterrence-based initiatives: A review of research. *Sultan Qaboos University Medical Journal,*11, 29–37.

Durrani, M., Waseem, H., Bhatti, J. A., Razzak, J. A. & Naseer, R. (2011). Associations of traffic safety attitudes and ticket fixing behaviours with the crash history of Pakistani drivers. *International Journal of Injury Control and Safety Promotion*, epub, 1–6, iFirst article.

Fernandes, R., Job, R. F. S. & Hatfield, J. (2004). Young drivers characteristics in the prediction of drinkdriving: Comparing drink-driving with a range of driving behaviours. Paper presented at the *International Council on Alcohol, Drugs and Traffic Safety.* Glasgow. from http://www.icadts.org/T2004/pdfs/O59.pdf

Fildes, B. N. & Lee, S. J. (1993). *The speed review: Road environment, behaviour, speed limits, enforcement and crashes, Report CR127.* Canberra: Federal Office of Road Safety.

Fleiter, J. J., Lennon, A. & Watson, B. (2007). Choosing not to speed: A qualitative exploration of differences in perceptions about speed limit compliance and related issues. Paper presented at the *Australasian Road*

Safety Research Policing Education Conference, Melbourne, 17-19 October. Melbourne.

Fleiter, J. J. & Watson, B. (2006). The speed paradox: the misalignment between driver attitudes and speeding behaviour. *Journal of the Australasian College of Road Safety, 17*(2), 23-30.

Fleiter, J. J., Watson, B., Lennon, A., King, M. J. & Shi, K. (2009). Speeding in Australia and China: A comparison of the influence of legal sanctions and enforcement practices on car drivers. Paper presented at the *Australasian Road Safety Research Policing Education Conference*. Sydney.

Fleiter, J. J., Watson, B., Lennon, A., King, M. J. & Shi, K. (2011). Social influences on drivers in China. *Journal of the Australasian College of Road Safety, 22*(2), 29-36.

Freeman, J., Liossis, P., Schonfeld, C., Sheehan, M., Siskind, V. & Watson, B. (2006). The self-reported impact of legal and non-legal sanctions on a group of recidivist drink drivers. *Transportation Research Part F, 9*, 53-64.

Gibbs, J. P. (1979). Assessing the deterrence doctrine: A challenge for the social and behavioral sciences. *American Behavioral Scientist, 22*, 653-677.

Hagland, M. & Aberg, L. (2002). Stability in drivers' speed choice. *Transportation Research Part F, 5*, 177-188.

Hatfield, J. & Fernandes, R. (2009). *The role of risk-propensity in the risky driving of younger and older drivers, Report No. 2009-002*: Department of Infrastructure, Transport, Regional Development and Local Government.

Homel, R. (1988). *Policing and punishing the drinking driver: A study of general and specific deterrence*. New York: Springer-Verlag.

Ipsos Social Research Institute (2013). *Driver Attitudes to Speed Enforcement: Austroads Publication No. AP-R433-13*.

Johnston, I. (2010). Beyond "best practice" road safety thinking and systems management - A case for culture change research. *Safety Science, 48*(9), 1175-1181.

Jonah, B. A. (1997). Sensation seeking and risky driving: A review and synthesis of the literature. *Accident Analysis and Prevention, 29*, 651-665.

Jonah, B. A., Thiessen, R. & Au-Yeung, E. (2001). Sensation seeking, risky driving and behavioral adaptation. *Accident Analysis and Prevention, 33*, 679-684.

Kleck, G., Sever, B., Li, S. & Gertz, M. (2005). The missing link in general deterrence research. *Criminology, 43*(3), 623-659.

Kline, R. B. (1998). *Principles and Practice of Structural Equation Modeling.* New York: Guilford Press.

Lajunen, T., & Summala, H. (2003). Can we trust self-reports of driving? Effects of impression management on driver behaviour questionnaire responses. *Transportation Research Part F, 6,* 97-107.

Lewis, I., Watson, B., White, K. M., & Elliott, B. (2013). The beliefs which influence young males to speed and strategies to slow them down: Informing the content of anti-speeding messages. *Psychology and Marketing,* in press.

Matthews, G., Desmond, P. A., Joyner, L., Carcary, B., & Gilliland, K. (1996). Validation of the Driver Stress Inventory and Driver Coping Questionnaire. Paper presented at the *2006 International Conference on Traffic and Transport Psychology,* Valencia, Spain.

McCartt, A. T., Mayhew, D. R., Braitman, K. A., Ferguson, S. A. & Simpson, H. M. (2009). Effects of Age and Experience on Young Driver Crashes: Review of Recent Literature. *Traffic Injury Prevention, 10*(3), 209-219.

McLean, A. J. (2012). Reflections on speed control from a public health perspective. *Journal of the Australasian College of Road Safety, 23*(3), 51-59.

Nagin, D. S. & Pogarsky, G. (2001). Integrating celerity, impulsivity, and extralegal sanction threats into a model of general deterrence: Theory and evidence. *Criminology, 39,* 865-891.

Palamara, P. G. & Stevenson, M. R. (2003). A longitudinal investigation of psychological risk factors for speeding offences among young motor car drivers, RR128. Crawley, WA: Injury Research Centre.

Patil, S. M., Shope, J. T., Raghunathan T, E. & Bingham, C. R. (2006). The role of personality characteristics in young adult driving. *Traffic Injury Prevention, 7*(4), 328-334.

Pennay, D. (2009). *Community attitudes to road safety - 2008 survey report.* Canberra.

Piquero, A. R. & Paternoster, R. (1998). An application of Stafford and Warr's reconceptualization of deterrence to drinking and driving. *Journal of Research in Crime and Delinquency, 35,* 3-39.

Piquero, A. R. & Pogarsky, G. (2002). Beyond Stafford and Warr's reconceptualization of deterrence: Personal and vicarious experiences, impulsivity, and offending behavior. *Journal of Research in Crime and Delinquency, 39,* 153-186.

Raftery, S. J., Kloeden, C. N. & Royals, J. (2013). *Safer speeds: an evaluation of public education materials - CASR REPORT SERIES CASR114*: Centre for Automotive Safety Research, The University of Adelaide.

Regan, M. A., Young, K., Triggs, T., Tomasevic, N., Mitsopoulos, E., Tierney, P., et al. (2007). Effects on driving performance of in-vehicle intelligent transport systems: Final results of the Australian TAC SafeCar project. *Journal of the Australasian College of Road Safety, 18*(1), 23-30.

Ross, H. L. (1982). *Deterring the drinking driver: Legal policy and social control*. Lexington, MA: Lexington Books.

Scott-Parker, B., Hyde, M. K., Watson, B. & King, M. J. (2013). Speeding by young novice drivers: What can personal characteristics and psychosocial theory add to our understanding. *Accident Analysis & Prevention, 50*, 242-250.

Scott-Parker, B., Watson, B. & King, M. J. (2009). Understanding the psychosocial factors influencing the risky behaviour of young drivers. *Transportation Research Part F: Traffic Psychology and Behaviour, 12*(6), 470-482.

Scott-Parker, B., Watson, B., & King, M. J. & Hyde, M. K (in press), Punishment avoidance and intentional risky driving behaviour: What are the implications for 'getting away with it'?. *Psychology of Punishment,* 2013.

Senserrick, T. (2009). Australian graduated driver licensing systems. *Journal of the Australasian College of Road Safety, 20*, 20-26.

Shuey, R. (2004). The Safety Camera Partnership in Victoria - Key Success Factors to Achieve Road Trauma Reduction for Speed Related Collisions. *2004 Year Book of the Australasian College of Road Safety - Road Safety Towards 2010*, 37-39.

Skinner, B. F. (1953). *Science and Human Behavior*. New York: Free Press.

Soole, D. W., Watson, B. & Fleiter, J. J. (2013). Effects of average speed enforcement on speed compliance and crashes: A review of the literature. *Accident Analysis & Prevention, 54*, 46-56.

Stafford, M. C. & Warr, M. (1993). A reconceptualization of general and specific deterrence. *Journal of Research in Crime and Delinquency, 30*, 123-125.

Sutherland, E. H. (1947). *Principles of Criminology* (4th ed.). Philadelphia: JB Lippincott.

Vingilis, E. R. (1990). A new look at deterrence. In R. J. Wilson & R. E. Mann (Eds.), *Drinking and driving: Advances in research and prevention*. New York: Guilford Press.

Watling, C., Freeman, J., Palk, G. R. & Davey, J. D. (2011). Sex, drugs, and deterrence: Applyng Stafford and Warr's reconceptualization of deterrence theory to drug driving across the genders. In N. M. R. Palmetti, J.P (Ed.), *Psychology of Punishment* (57-71): Nova Science Publishers, Inc.

Watsford, R. (2008). The success of the 'Pinkie campaign - Speeding. No one thinks big of you: A new approach to road safety marketing. Paper presented at the *High Risk Road Users - motivating behaviour change: What works and what doesn't work? 2008 Joint ACRS-Travelsafe National Conference.* Brisbane: Australasian College of Road Safety. from http://www.acrs.org.au/srcfiles/Watsford.pdf.

Watson, B. (2004). *The psychosocial characteristics and on-road behaviour of unlicensed drivers.* Doctoral dissertation, Queensland University of Technology, Brisbane.

Watson, B., Siskind, V., Fleiter, J. J. & Watson, A. (2010). Different approaches to measuring specific deterrence: Some examples from speeding offender management. Paper presented at the *Australasian Road Safety Research, Policing and Education Conference.* Canberra, Australia.

Weatherburn, D. & Moffatt, S. (2011). The specific deterrent effect of higher fines on drink-driving offenders. *British Journal of Criminology, 51,* 789-803.

Whelan, M., Scully, J. & Newstead, S. (2009). *Vehicle safety and young drivers Stage 2 and 3: Analysis of young driver crash types and vehilce choice optimisation: Report 292*: Monash University Accident Research Centre.

World Health Organization (2013). *Global Status Report on Road Safety 2013: Supporting a Decade of Action.* Geneva.

Yu, J. (2000). Punishment and alcohol problems recidivism among drink-driving offenders. *Journal of Criminal Justice, 28,* 261-270.

In: Psychology of Punishment
Editor: Nicolas Castro

ISBN: 978-1-62948-103-6
© 2013 Nova Science Publishers, Inc.

Chapter 2

DIFFERENCES IN THE PROCESS OF CHOOSING CAPITAL PUNISHMENT OR IMPRISONMENT: EXCERPTS FROM A STUDY BY A JAPANESE LAY JUDGE

Eiichiro Watamura[1,3,*] *and Toshihiro Wakebe*[2,3]

[1]Department of Psychology, Keio University,
Mita, Minato-ku, Tokyo, Japan
[2]Department of Cognitive Neuroscience, Graduate School of Medicine,
The University of Tokyo. Hongo, Bunkyo-ku, Tokyo, Japan
[3]Japan Society for the Promotion of Science

ABSTRACT

The purpose of this study is to clarify the difference between decision-making processes that result in capital punishment and other forms of punishment, as made by lay judges in Japan. In this study, 126 Japanese undergraduate students listened to an audio recording of a fictitious murder trial and were asked to determine a punishment for the defendant ranging from several years' imprisonment to the death penalty. They were then split into two groups according to whether they chose the death penalty or not. This was followed by a comprehensive comparison of the verdicts of the two groups covering every angle. The results show

* Phone: +81-3-5841-3861, Fax: +81-3-5841-8969, E-mail: eiichiro@L.u-tokyo.ac.jp.

that members of the group that chose the death penalty were already in favor of it before the study, and that the group that chose the death penalty evaluated the arguments and mitigating evidence in the trial in a disadvantageous way for the defendant. Finally, the most significant finding was that the group favoring the death penalty cited deterrence and retribution as reasons for their decision, while the group favoring imprisonment cited rehabilitation and retribution. A majority of earlier studies have shown that ordinary citizens do not consider deterrence and retribution together when determining punishment, while awarding the death penalty involves the consideration of both, which causes stress and anxiety for the lay judge. This study demonstrates that, in order to free themselves of this burden, lay judges likely justify death penalty decisions by reminding themselves that it deters crime in addition to its retributive purpose.

The ultimate punishment for a criminal defendant is the death penalty, also known as capital punishment. In a worldwide trend, fewer and fewer countries are now carrying out executions (Amnesty, 2012). Nevertheless, some countries—including the most advanced, such as the Unites States and Japan—consistently uphold capital punishment. The crimes to which the death penalty applies in those countries are those specified by law as the most serious. For instance, capital punishment can be applied to those defendants accused of first-degree murder involving the most heinous types of crimes, such as rape, arson, or multiple murders. However, the death penalty is not always applied to those crimes. In the case of first-degree murder, defendants can be sentenced to life without parole, escaping the death penalty. Even if it is hardly probable that a defendant will be freed, a life sentence is definitely different from the death penalty. Defendants who are sentenced to death often abandon themselves to despair for the rest of their lives. On the other hand, those sentenced to life without parole are not quite hopeless, even though they are not allowed to live a free life in the community. They can at least escape from the fear of death. This difference leads us to the simple conclusion that the decision of whether or not to sentence a defendant to death is a crucial one.

Appellate courts, judges, and attorneys also admit that murder trials are special among ordinal criminal trials (SunWolf, 2007). As the decision-making process for the death penalty cannot be undermined even slightly, it is necessary to eliminate arbitrariness and disparity from punishment decisions in courts in which laypeople determine other peoples' punishment (Sporer & Goodman-Delahunty, 2009). Therefore, we cannot rule out the possibility that a death-row inmate could be sentenced to life without parole if he or she were to be judged by different people. This raises the question: what are the differences in the decision-making process when the same case results in either the death penalty or imprisonment?

PREVIOUS RESEARCH ON CAPITAL PUNISHMENT

Over the past decades, a considerable number of studies have been conducted on capital punishment around the world. However, little attention has been given to murder trials in studies targeting places in which the death penalty has been abolished or suspended, such as Europe or Australia. This is probably because these regions have already lost the opportunity to provide death sentences. Research about decision making in murder trials hardly makes sense in their judicial systems as long as the research setting is unrealistic. Naturally, studies in these regions have mainly focused on "peoples" attitudes towards the capital punishment system. Interestingly, studies have found that a portion of people in these regions strongly support the death penalty, even when the death penalty is illegal and its restoration is very unlikely (e.g., Forsterlee, Horowitz, Forsterlee, King, & Ronlund, 1999; Hessing, Keijser, & Elffers, 2003; Unnever & Cullen, 2010). In the Netherlands, for example, although the percentage of people who support the death penalty has persisted at the 30-40% level since the death penalty was formally abolished in 1983, some people who regard crime as a serious threat and who are disaffected by the government strongly support the death penalty (Hessing et al., 2003). In almost all European countries, those who are intolerant of racial minority groups are more positive about the death penalty (Unnever & Cullen, 2010). Moreover, Forsterlee et al. (1999) revealed that 71% of young people in Australia support the death penalty, which was abolished there in 1985. It seems that attitudes toward the death penalty are relevant to decision making: those who support the death penalty tend to choose it in actual trials (Allen, Mabry, & McKelton, 1998; O'Neil, Patry, & Penrod, 2004). However, little is known about what differs in the decision-making process when the same case is judged to require death or not.

In contrast, studies of the United States, which has retained capital punishment, have focused on trial decision making in relation to attitudes toward the death penalty. In these studies, two kinds of factors have been investigated: demographics and religious/political ideology. Demographic factors includes jurors' sex, race, age, and marital status. With some exceptions, males are more likely than females to choose the death penalty

(Beckham, Spray, & Pietz, 2007; Lynch & Haney, 2009; O'Neil et al., 2004; Sandys & McGarrell, 1995; Watson, Ross, & Morris, 2003; Whitehead & Blankenship, 2000). White people more willingly choose the death penalty than non-white people (Baker, Lambert, & Jenkins, 2005; Lynch & Haney, 2009; Maggard, Payne, & Chappell, 2012; Unnever & Cullen, 2007). Middle-aged and older people tend to choose the death penalty more often than younger people (Fox, Radelet, & Bonsteel, 1990; Stack, 2000), while married people are more likely to choose it than single people (Bohm, 2003; Maggard et al., 2012). As far as religion and political ideology, according to the studies of O'Neil et al. (2004) and Miller and Haney (2009), Protestants are more willing to choose the death penalty than Catholics, while Conservatives are more likely to choose the death penalty than liberals (Baumer, Messner, & Rosenfeld, 2003; Jacobs & Carmichael, 2004; Jacobs, Carmichael, & Kent, 2005; McCann, 2008; Platania & Moran, 1999).

The studies of the United States are valid in the investigation of whether these factors decrease the fairness of murder trials. Furthermore, they are helpful for the qualification of jurors in actual trials. However, two important problems still remain in these studies of the United States. First, they do not sufficiently address our research question regarding what differs in the decision-making process when the same case is awarded either the death penalty or imprisonment. As was discussed earlier, demographic, religious, and political factors tend to influence death penalty decisions. However, this finding is not robust. Some studies have failed to indicate these results, or have even indicated contrary results. Sex and age are good examples of factors that differ from study to study. Although most studies have shown that males are more likely than females to choose the death penalty (e.g., Beckham et al., 2007), some indicated no difference between the sexes (Lester, Maggioncalda-Aretz, & Stark, 1997; Vallient & Oliver, 1997). Similarly, young people have been found to be more supportive of the death penalty, contrary to the studies mentioned above (Lester et al., 1997; O' Neil et al., 2004). Even more complex is the interaction between other factors. Although whites are more likely than blacks to choose the death penalty, the reverse is true in cases where the defendant is white (Mitchell, Haw, Pfeifer, & Meissner, 2005). Even if they are Protestant, females are still not likely to choose the death penalty (Miller & Hayward, 2008). It is therefore difficult to determine what is different in the decision-making processes when the defendant is sentenced to death and when he or she is not, even in the same case. The chaotic state of previous research suggests that we need to shift our perspective on this question.

It is now necessary to pay attention to the essential factors that influence death penalty decisions. In other words, we need to focus on the differences in a decision-making process in which demographic, religious, and ideological factors are almost homogeneous. In addition, decision-making in capital trials has hardly been studied outside the United States, although a number of other countries still retain the death penalty and some give ordinary citizens the opportunity to choose it. In order to understand the death sentence decision-making process without a cultural and institutional framework, it is necessary to verify this process in the capital trials of other countries.

Japan is the only G8 country besides the United States that retains the death penalty. These two countries are also similar in that ordinary citizens have the opportunity to choose the death penalty. In light of this and the aforementioned issues, we conducted a survey of Japanese undergraduates. The group was homogeneous in many demographic factors, such as race, age, and education, though not in sex. Moreover, most Japanese people do not adhere to a particular religion (Miller, 1998)[1] and rarely come in conflict with each other ideologically because of the long single regime of the Liberal Democratic Party, which has been in power since the Second World War. Therefore, this survey of Japanese undergraduates will enable us to focus on differences in the decision-making process alone.

THE DEATH PENALTY IN JAPAN

According to UNODC (2012), in Japan, the annual homicide rate per 100,000 people in 2011 was 0.35. This number is considerably low compared with Germany (0.81), France (1.09), the United Kingdom (1.23), the United States (4.7), and Canada (1.70).[2] Compared with East Asian countries such as China (1.12), South Korea (2.9), and Taiwan (3.0), Japan's rate is much lower. Japan is considered a relatively low security risk. Yet, despite this very low risk, most Japanese people support the death penalty. According to a survey carried out by the Cabinet Office in December 2009, 85.6% of citizens answered "yes" to the question, "Do you approve of death penalty?" while only 5.7% said "no" (Cabinet Office, 2009). This result indicates that Japan is

---

[1] In fact, Japan has mixed religious traditions: they enjoy Christmas in December, pay their respects to a Shinto shrine at the beginning of the year, and hold funeral rites in the Buddhist style.

[2] The statistics on China are from 2008, France and South Korea from 2009, and the United Kingdom and Taiwan from 2010. All others are from 2011.

extraordinarily affirmative about the death penalty as a matter of national character. The crimes applicable to the death penalty are the most serious ones that involve taking a life, such as murder, death on the occasion of a robbery, or death by arson.[3] A deliberation group made up of three professional judges and six lay judges makes the sentencing decision. After a trial of several days or more, the group determines both the verdict and the sentence for the defendant. From May 2009, when the lay judge system was begun, to March 2013, 17 death sentences have been passed in Japan.

Besides the fact that professional judges participate in the deliberation, Japanese murder trials are different from those in the United States in two ways. First, the death sentence is not determined by a unanimous vote. On the condition that at least one professional judge agrees, it is determined by majority vote in principle. In other words, if more than five judges, including at least one professional judge, approve the death sentence decision, the defendant will be executed. Second, what is profoundly different from American trials is that the death penalty is always one of the choices in Japanese murder trials. For instance, the punishments applicable to murder in Japan are the death penalty, life imprisonment, or more than five years' imprisonment. Japanese lay judges in a murder case are required to choose one of these by considering the evidence with professional judges. Even in a murder case, they can choose five years imprisonment or even a suspended sentence if the defendant killed his or her family because of caregiver fatigue, while they can choose the death penalty when the case leaves no room for leniency, such as random killing. Unlike murder trials in the United States, it is not only the death penalty and life imprisonment that are discussed in Japan. The death penalty is one candidate among a wide range of punishments.

THE PRESENT STUDY

In this study, after listening to an audio file depicting an imaginary murder trial, the participants were asked to play the part of lay judges by choosing one of three punishments: the death penalty, life imprisonment, and more than five years imprisonment. They also answered several questions, which were closely relevant to the punishment decision-making process. We compared the

---

[3] Although the death penalty is also applicable to civil commotion crimes and instigation of foreign aggression crimes, these crimes have hardly occurred since World War II.

responses of the group that chose the death penalty with those of the group that chose other punishments. There were four categories of questions, as follows.

The first category related to attitudes toward the death penalty. We used the Japanese translation of Jones & Wiener's Death Qualification Scale (2011). Participants were asked to choose one of the following four statements.

1. If the defendant were found guilty of a murder for which the law allowed a death sentence, I would always vote to sentence the defendant to death even if the facts in the case did not show that the defendant deserved a death sentence.
2. I am in favor of the death penalty, but I would not necessarily vote for it in every case in which the law allowed it. I would consider the facts of the particular case that pertain to the death penalty and then decide whether to sentence the defendant to death.
3. Although I have doubts about the death penalty, I would be able to find the defendant guilty and to vote for a death sentence when the law allowed it, if the facts of the case showed that the defendant was guilty and should be given a death sentence.
4. I have such strong doubts about the death penalty that I would be unable to find the defendant guilty and vote for a death sentence when the law allowed it, even if the facts of the case showed that the defendant was guilty and deserved a death sentence.

The first statement reflects a strongly affirmative attitude toward the death penalty, while the last reflects a very strong attitude to the contrary. Those who are affirmative have a tendency to choose a death sentence (Allen, et al., 1998; O'Neil et al, 2004). In our study, it was expected that the death sentence group would be more affirmative than the group that chose other sentences.

The second category involved the evaluation of the arguments and evidence in the trial. In our study, the participants were asked to rate how convincing the arguments of the prosecutor and the defense attorney were on a five-point scale. According to previous studies, those who chose the death penalty should be more sympathetic to the prosecutor but less sympathetic to the defense attorney than those who did not (Fitzgerald & Ellsworth, 1984; Thompson, Cowan, Ellsworth, & Harrington, 1984, Poulson, Braithwaite, Brondino, & Wuensch, 1997).

Additionally, our participants were asked to rate how they would accept two pieces of mitigating evidence on a five-point scale. Those who preferred the death penalty to life without parole evaluated the evidence in a disadvantageous manner for the defendant. On the basis of these findings, we predicted that the death sentence group would regard the prosecutor's argument as more convincing while regarding the defense attorney's argument as less convincing and at the same time denying the mitigating evidence.

The third category regarded confidence in the respondents' own decisions. Analyses of the juror decision-making process in murder trials have exposed jurors' severe stress and anxiety after making their decisions. In Costanzo and Costanzo's (1994) study, the experienced jurors who chose the death penalty had thought over their decisions and then settled on ideas that cleared them of stress and anxiety, such as, "I am not the final judge of the defendant," or "My sentence will not be carried out." This result indicates that jurors who chose the death penalty were not confident in their decision. Thus, in our study, the death sentence group was expected to rate lower than the other group on items such as, "My decision was right."

The last category related to the reason for the punishment decision. Previous studies have classified reasons that justify criminal punishment into four theoretical types: retribution, incapacitation, rehabilitation, and deterrence (e.g., Carlsmith, 2006). Retribution is the theory that criminal defendants should pay for what they have done, which is also called "an eye for an eye" justice.

Incapacitation is a theory that aims at social safety by isolating defendants from society by means of punishment, while rehabilitation regards punishment as the means of improving defendants' behavior to achieve the same goal. Deterrence theory uses punishment as a warning to prevent people from committing crimes. In general crime settings, ordinary citizens determine punishment on the grounds of retribution (Carlsmith, 2006; Carlsmith, Darley, & Robinson, 2002; Darley, Carlsmith, & Robinson, 2000; Keller, Oswald, & Stucki, 2010; Rucker, Polifroni, Tetlock, & Scott, 2004; Watamura, Wakebe, & Takano, 2010), while incapacitation, rehabilitation, and deterrence are not generally considered. Above all, deterrence is rarely cited as a reason for decision-making.

However, very few empirical attempts have been made to determine whether or not this tendency also applies to the special crime setting of death sentences. For what reason the decision is made is the most important issue in this study because it is very close to the determination of punishment. We have therefore tried to identify the differences in decision-making processes that result in either the death penalty or other sentences from a new angle using the aforementioned four categories of questions.

METHOD

Tasks

Participants were required to answer several questions, including the final punishment decision, after listening to an audio recording depicting a criminal trial.

Participants

The participants were 126 undergraduates from Sensyu University in Tokyo: 90 male, 35 female, and one unknown. Their average age was 19 (SD=1.0). During a lecture on the liberal arts, we carried out our survey with those who agreed to participate arbitrarily in a group setting.

Materials

The material used in the study was an audio file depicting an imaginary murder case. It was approximately 25 minutes long. A brief summary of the case is as follows.

The defendant (male, 23) had a spirited quarrel with the victim (male, 55) in a bar after they bumped into each other in front of the restroom. Feeling an increasing anger, the defendant came at the victim with the aid of an accomplice when the victim left the bar, and unleashed a fierce attack that resulted in the victim's death.

The scenario was closely modeled on an actual murder case. Four members of an amateur theatrical group were employed and cast as the judge, the prosecutor, the defense attorney, and the defendant. The audio file was recorded in a sound booth. The first half included the opening statement read by the judge, the indictment and argument read by the prosecutor, and the defense attorney's statement. The last half of the recording contained the questions to the defendant and the prosecutor's and defense attorney's closing statements.

The defendant had already been proven guilty in this case. In the Japanese lay judge system, as in other countries' civil participation systems, the verdict is determined before the punishment decision. However, as the focus of our study was not the verdict but the punishment decision, we omitted the verdict procedure. The prosecutor stressed the vital need for severe punishment, while the defense attorney argued against severe punishment on the grounds that the defendant had taken mind-altering drugs and alcohol at that time he committed the murder. Regardless of the defense attorney's argument, we predicted that a large proportion of the participants would choose the death penalty, putting more emphasis on the cruel fact that two men assaulted another to death.

The file was played on a personal computer through the audio equipment in the lecture room.

Questionnaire and Question Items

The questionnaire consisted of nine pages. The first page contained an explanation of the survey purpose, a request for voluntary cooperation, and gender and age boxes. The purpose was explained as a survey of young people's attitudes toward criminal punishment, keeping secret our true purpose of comparing the death sentence group with the imprisonment group (they were debriefed about this on a different day). The second page contained the Japanese translation of the Death Qualification Scale. On the third page, we explained how to answer the punishment question. The participants were asked to choose one of three possibilities: death penalty, life imprisonment, and more than five years imprisonment. They were urged to answer seriously, as if they were the lay judges in the case. The fourth and sixth pages contained boxes for making notes when listening to the first and second half of the audio file. The participants were free to refer to these notes when answering questions later.

The fifth page contained items asking for evaluations of the argument and mitigating evidence at end of the first half of the trial. Participants were required to rate how convincing the prosecutor's and defense attorney's arguments each were on a five-point Likert scale (1: unconvincing, 5: convincing). They were also required to rate the mitigating evidence on a five-point Likert scale (1: disagree, 5: agree) for the following two items.

1. What caused the defendant to kill the victim was mind-altering drugs and alcohol.
2. The defendant had no intention to kill the victim.

On the seventh page, we provided four categories of questions. The first, which was the most important in this study, was the punishment decision. The participants were asked which of the three sentences would be the most appropriate for this defendant. If they chose more than five years imprisonment, they were asked to say how many years they felt were appropriate.

The second question regarded their confidence in their decisions. The participants were requested to rate two statements—"My punishment decision is right" and "My punishment decision will gain popular acceptance"—on a five-point Likert scale (1: disagree, 5: agree). The third question asked again for their evaluations of the prosecutor's and defense attorney's arguments, as well as the mitigating evidence, now that that they had heard the end of the trial. In the same way as on the fifth page, they evaluated how convincing both sides' arguments were and how much they approved of the effects of mind-altering drugs and alcohol and lack of intent to kill.

Finally, the last question asked about the reason for their punishment decision. The participants were asked to rate how appropriate the following four reasons were for their decision-making regarding the punishment of the defendant.

1. To isolate or dismiss a dangerous defendant from society (incapacitation)
2. To give the defendant what he deserves (retribution)
3. To make the defendant reflect on his misconduct and rehabilitate him (rehabilitation)
4. To prevent other evil people from committing crimes (deterrence)

The participants rated each item on a five-point Likert scale (1: inappropriate, 5: appropriate).

Procedure

After a lecture on the liberal arts, we asked the credited undergraduates to participate in our survey at their own discretion. The survey was conducted in the same lecture room. After filling out the gender and age boxes on the first page, the participants filled out the Death Qualification Scale. Next, they were told how to answer the punishment question.

As in the questionnaire, they were urged to answer seriously, as if they were the lay judges in the case. After listening to the first half of the trial, they answered the questions on the fifth page about the arguments and mitigating evidence. Soon after, they listened to the second half of the trial and answered the rest of the questions. The survey took about 40 minutes to be completed by all of the participants. They were given a report of the results on a different day.

RESULTS

Before the analysis, data on six participants were excluded because they had missing values in the questionnaire. The remaining 120 participants' questionnaires were examined.

Eleven students chose the death penalty, 41 chose life imprisonment, and 68 chose more than five years imprisonment. The average length of punishment chosen by the third group was 17.1 years. We had predicted that a large proportion of the participants would choose the death penalty in this trial because of the cruelty of the crime. Contrary to our prediction, only 10% chose the death penalty.

We divided the data into two groups, the death sentence group and the imprisonment group, and compared the two. In terms of the Death Qualification Scale, the mean rating of the death sentence group was lower than that of the imprisonment group (1.73 vs. 2.30). Mann-Whitney's U test revealed a significant difference between the groups ($p<.01$). A low rating on this ordinal scale means that a participant has an affirmative attitude toward the death penalty. As predicted, the people in the death sentence group were already very affirmative toward the death penalty.

In the next stage, we examined the evaluations of the arguments made by the prosecutor and the defense attorney. The participants rated them twice, after listening to the first and the second halves of the trial, based on how convincing their arguments were, on a five-point Likert scale (1: not convincing, 5: convincing). The results are shown in Table 1. We conducted a 2X2X2 analysis of variance (group: death sentence vs. imprisonment; target: prosecutor vs. defense attorney; evaluation point: after the first half vs. after the second half). This analysis revealed a significant group X target interaction (F (1, 118) =16.3, $p<.001$), as well as main effects for both group (F (1,118) = 4.6, $p=.03$) and target (F (1,118) = 82.8, $p<.001$).

Figure 1. shows the results of the group X target interaction. The prosecutor was seen as more convincing than the defense attorney overall (4.1 vs. 3.0). This difference was significant in both the death sentence group and the imprisonment group ($ps<.001$).

Table 1. Mean ratings of prosecution and defense arguments（SD）

Group	Target	First half		Last half	
Death	Prosecurtor	4.5	(0.52)	4.5	(0.52)
	Attorney	2.2	(1.17)	1.8	(0.87)
Other	Prosecurtor	4.0	(0.72)	4.2	(0.79)
	Attorney	3.2	(1.11)	3.1	(1.14)

What is more remarkable here is the comparison between these two groups: the main effect was that the total rating (prosecutor plus defense attorney) was somewhat lower in the death sentence group than in the imprisonment group (3.3 vs. 3.6). This indicates that the death sentence group was skeptical about all of the arguments in the trial, whether made by the prosecutor or the defense attorney. In the evaluations of the prosecutor alone, however, the death sentence group regarded the argument as more convincing than the imprisonment group (4.5 vs. 4.1, p=.03).

In contrast, the rating of the defense attorney by the death sentence group was remarkably lower than that of the imprisonment group (2.0 vs. 3.1, p<0001), indicating that they did not regard the defense attorney's argument as convincing. Therefore, it would be better to say that this asymmetric evaluation resulted in the group's main effect, rather than that the death sentence group was skeptical. In the meantime, the evaluation point had neither a main effect nor an interaction effect. This indicates that the tendency of the death-sentence group to consider the prosecutor's argument more convincing than the defense attorney's argument, in contrast with the imprisonment group, was consistent throughout the trial.

The participants were also asked to evaluate twice—after the first and second halves of the trial—two items about mitigating evidence on a five-point Likert scale (1: disagree, 5: agree). With regard to the item, "What caused the defendant to kill the victim was mind-altering drugs and alcohol," the ratings after listening to the first half and the second half showed little difference in both the death sentence group (1.8 vs. 1.7) and the imprisonment group (2.5 vs. 2.2).

A 2X2 analysis of variance (group: death sentence vs. imprisonment; evaluation point: after the first half vs. after the second half) revealed the main effect of the group (F (1,118) =4.4, p=.04), indicating that the death sentence group refused to admit the evidence. While it was not significant, the ratings on the other item, "The defendant had no intention to kill the victim," were rather lower in the death sentence group (M_{pre}=2.0$\supset M_{post}$=2.1) than in the imprisonment group (M_{pre}=2.6$\supset M_{post}$=2.3). Nevertheless, it seems quite clear that the death sentence group was less likely to accept the mitigating evidence than the imprisonment group.

Contrary to our prediction, the members of the death sentence group were more confident in their decisions than those of the imprisonment group. After choosing the punishment, the participants were asked to respond to the items, "My punishment decision is right" and "My punishment decision will gain popular acceptance" on a five-point Likert scale (1: disagree, 5: agree).

For the first statement, the mean rating of the death sentence group was 3.9, while that of the imprisonment group was 3.2, showing a significant difference (t (118) =2.62, p<.01).

For the second statement, the rating was also somewhat higher in the death sentence group than in the imprisonment group (3.4 vs. 3.1), but the difference was not significant. It could be understood from these results that the death sentence group had more confidence in the decision itself, without being so sure whether other people would praise their decision to sentence the defendant to death.

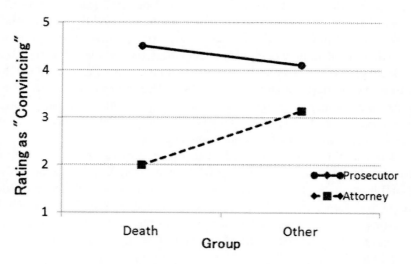

Note: The evaluations of points (after the first half vs. after the second half) was collapsed because there was no difference between them.

Figure 1. Mean ratings of prosecution and defense.

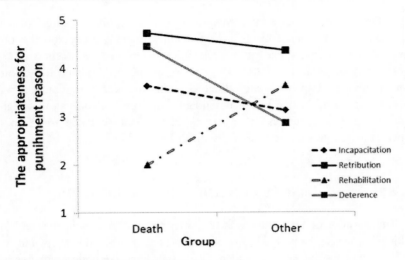

Figure 2. Mean ratings of reasons for punishment.

Finally, the reasons for the punishment decision were examined. The participants rated the appropriateness of each reason—incapacitation, retribution, rehabilitation, and deterrence—on a five-point Likert scale (1: inappropriate, 5: appropriate). The results are shown in Figure 2. The death sentence group and the imprisonment group both rated retribution as the most appropriate reason for their decisions. The ratings on incapacitation were little different. However, the death sentence group and the imprisonment group were completely reversed regarding the other two reasons, rehabilitation and deterrence. The death sentence group rated deterrence as the second most appropriate reason and rehabilitation as the least appropriate. In contrast, the imprisonment group regarded rehabilitation as the second most appropriate reason and deterrence as the least. A 2X4 analysis (group: death sentence vs. imprisonment; reason: incapacitation vs. retribution vs. rehabilitation vs. deterrence) revealed the interaction and main effects of the reason (F (3,354) =15.0, $p<.001$, F (3,354) =13.1, $p<.001$, respectively).

As a result of multiple comparisons, we found that the rating of deterrence was significantly higher in the death sentence group than in the imprisonment group, while that of rehabilitation was significantly higher in the imprisonment group than in the death sentence group ($ps<.001$).

By group, all of the pairs except for retribution-deterrence were significantly different in the death sentence group ($ps<.001$). This means that they chose the death penalty in order to do justice to the defendant and at the same time to decrease crime. Meanwhile, they hardly expected that the defendant would remake his life. In the imprisonment group, on the other hand, all of the pairs except incapacitation-deterrence were shown to be significantly different ($ps<.001$). Their main reason for choosing life or more than five years imprisonment coincided with the death sentence group's reason, to provide justice to the defendant. However, rehabilitation weighed heavily in their decision, as deterrence did in the death sentence group. In this respect, the two groups were critically different.

DISCUSSION AND CONCLUSION

The purpose of this study was to clarify the differences in the decision-making processes involved in choosing either the death penalty or imprisonment for the same defendant. Targeting Japanese undergraduates who were almost homogeneous in many factors—including race, age, education, religion, and political ideology—enabled us to focus on the essential factors that determine whether someone chooses the death penalty or not. The study was expected to provide a resource for understanding decision-making processes in capital trials outside the United States.

Contrary to our expectations, only 10% of the participants chose the death penalty after listening to a recording of a mock murder trial, regardless of the cruelty of the crime. One interpretation of this result is that the participants might have chosen their sentences very carefully because they were asked, in both verbal and written instructions, to choose a sentence as if they were actual lay judges in the trial. This strict instruction might have prevented them from engaging in easy decision making, including thoughts such as, "Maybe another punishment is better, but the death penalty is not wrong," so a small proportion of them chose the death penalty.

To return to our main concern, we successfully found several important differences between the death sentence group and the imprisonment group. The first was a difference in their original attitudes toward the death penalty. We translated Jones and Wiener's Death Qualification Scale (2011) into Japanese and asked all of the participants to answer it before the audio file was played. Consistent with previous studies (Allen, et al., 1998; O'Neil et al, 2004), the result showed that the members of the death sentence group were more affirmative toward the death penalty than those of the imprisonment group, suggesting that they were not reluctant to sentence the defendant to death.

A second difference was found in the evaluations of the arguments and mitigating evidence in the trial. According to Fitzgerald and Ellsworth (1984), Thompson et al. (1984), and Poulson et al. (1997), those who choose the death penalty are more sympathetic to the prosecutor and less sympathetic to the defense attorney than those who do not. Lynch and Haney (2009) and Poulson et al. (1997) also demonstrated that those who choose the death penalty are more likely to evaluate evidence in a way that is disadvantageous for the defendant, disregarding childhood abuse or mental disease as mitigating factors. These findings led us to examine the differences in the evaluation of the prosecutor's and defense attorney's arguments as well as the mitigating evidence.

The evaluation was measured twice: after the first half of the audio recording and after the second half. As predicted, a clear difference was found between the two groups regarding the evaluation of the arguments. The prosecutor's argument was considered more convincing by the death sentence group than by the imprisonment group, while the defense attorney's argument was considered dramatically less convincing by the death sentence group. More remarkably, this evaluation of the arguments did not differ from the first half to the second half of the trial. The death sentence group was consistently pro-prosecutor and anti-defense attorney throughout the trial.

This unbalanced evaluation was similarly found regarding the mitigating evidence. In our study's trial, two pieces of mitigating evidence were presented: "What caused the defendant to kill the victim was mind-altering drugs and alcohol" and "The defendant had no intention to kill the victim." Although we could not find a significant difference regarding the latter statement, the death sentence group was more skeptical and evaluated both pieces of evidence disadvantageously for the defendant. Interestingly, as with the evaluation of the arguments, this evaluation of the mitigating evidence was consistent throughout the trial. These results suggest that the process of choosing the death sentence was fundamentally different from the process of choosing imprisonment in the way participants evaluated the arguments and evidence in the trial. Those who chose the death penalty saw all of what was presented in the trial as negative from beginning to end. This may be considered a kind of bias affecting legal decision making.

Finally, the most important difference was found in the reason for each participant's decision. Previous studies have repeatedly shown that the ordinal citizen's determination of punishment is based on retribution in principle, while other reasons are comparatively ignored (Carlsmith, 2006; Keller et al., 2010; Rucker et al., 2004; Sunstein, 2000). Above all, deterrence is considered less importance than incapacitation, rehabilitation, and retribution (Carlsmith, 2006). In our study, retribution was rated as the most appropriate reason, in line with previous studies. This part of the result was common between the death sentence group and the imprisonment group. However, the death-sentence group regarded deterrence as slightly less appropriate than retribution. In this point, our study differed completely from previous studies.

One explanation for this is that the participants in our study were Japanese, in contrast with previous studies of American people. Differences in culture or institution might cause them to have different reasons for punishment. However, one previous study of Japanese people also showed that they found deterrence to be the least appropriate reason for punishment (Watamura et al., 2010). Furthermore, the group that chose life or more than five years imprisonment rated deterrence as the least appropriate reason for their decision, which was consistent with previous studies. These findings suggest that placing emphasis on deterrence along with retribution is specific to death penalty decision making. This may come from the justification brought about by the deterrence theory. Given that retribution has been proven to be the only reason for punishment decision making after filtering previous findings (Carlsmith, 2006), all of the other reasons are post hoc and merely used to justify the decision afterward (Haidt, 2001). In particular, the choice of the death penalty can cause stress and anxiety because it means taking the defendant's life (Costanzo & Costanzo, 1994). Retribution that aims at giving justice to the defendant is not enough of a reason to choose the death penalty. This might urge us to attend to deterrence in order to ease this stress and anxiety by justifying that the death penalty is not only retributively just, but also effective in deterring other crimes.

Our interpretation that deterrence is specific to death penalty decision making is supported by the confidence of our participants. In our study, the death sentence group was more likely to think, "My punishment decision is right." Although they were not sure whether their decision would gain popular acceptance, they had great confidence in the decision itself. This was clearly contrary to our prediction, since death penalty decision making, as mentioned above, is often accompanied by stress and anxiety (Costanzo & Costanzo, 1994). The members of the death sentence group successfully eased their stress and anxiety by justifying their decision—"The death penalty will prevent other people from committing crimes and benefit society in the future"—and they can therefore have confidence in that decision. On the other hand, rehabilitation, which aims at the defendant's reflection and improvement, was considered the least important of all four reasons by the death sentence group, while it was considered second only to retribution by the imprisonment group. These findings indicate that death penalty decision making is quite different from decision making regarding other punishments, even if the original reason for both is retribution.

Suggestions for Actual Trials

This study yields two important suggestions for actual trials. First, whether or not the death penalty is chosen considerably depends on the composition of the lay judges. Our study revealed that people who are predisposed to support the death penalty are more likely to choose it when determining the results of a trial. This means that the same case will be sentenced quite differently depending on whether the majority of judges are affirmative of or resistant to the death penalty. In order to decrease this risk and ensure fairness, the careful selection of judges or jurors based on the Death Qualification Scale, as exercised in American murder trials, is considered essential. Yet, the Japanese lay judge system has no alternative to this scale because the death penalty is only one choice of punishment for serious crimes such as murder. In other words, Japanese serious crime trials do not focus only on whether or not the defendant should be sentenced to death.

Aside from this problem, what is more serious in the Japanese lay judge system is the majority vote principle. It is therefore very likely that the final sentence will be different depending on the trial judges, even in the same case. The Japanese lay judge system should take these risks seriously and consider ways in which to remove the influence of the composition of the lay judges by referencing the jury system of the United States.

The second suggestion, which is valid for all legal systems in which ordinary citizens have the opportunity to choose the death penalty, is that without careful consideration those citizens should not be given information that can justify the death penalty. In this study, the participants who chose the death penalty gave deterrence as the primary reason for their decision, while deterrence is almost ignored in ordinary citizens' determination of punishment (Carlsmith, 2006). As was discussed earlier, the concept of deterrence might ease stress and anxiety by serving as justification that the death penalty is beneficial for social safety. In actual trials, however, deterrence is not the only reason for which people justify their decisions. For instance, jurors' or lay judges' insistence on the death penalty may lead them to the idea, "I was persuaded into choosing the death penalty, so I am not responsible," or the information that the defendant desperately wants to be sentenced to death might justify the death penalty and ease stress and anxiety.

As mentioned in the opening section, the death penalty is the ultimate punishment because it involves taking a life and is irreversible. Therefore, the death penalty should be chosen more carefully than any other criminal punishment. Considering that some information can justify the death penalty easily without forcing the jurors or lay judges to scrutinize the arguments and evidence, access to such information should be limited by proper legal processes, such as asking the jurors or lay judges to express their decision before hearing others' opinions, or to instruct them to ignore the defendant's thoughts and behaviors.

FUTURE RESEARCH

This study targeted Japanese undergraduates who were almost homogeneous in race, age, education, religion, and political ideology. This successfully enabled us to focus on the differences in decision-making processes without interference. However, our findings are perhaps not always true of the actual trials. In Japan, ordinary citizens, who are more heterogeneous than those in our study, are appointed as lay judges. Future studies need to make sure that death penalty decision-making remains different from other punishment decisions even with these other factors involved. It will also be useful to compare death penalty decision making internationally. These investigations will deepen our understanding of decisions regarding the death penalty, regardless of the framework of cultures and institutions.

Our study lacked some essential procedures that are present in actual trials. The first of these was the deliberation process. Usually, the final sentence is not determined by an individual, but by the deliberation of a group of jurors or lay judges, and sometimes professional judges, within the civil participation system, including the American jury system and the Japanese lay judge system. During the deliberation process, those who think that the death penalty is appropriate at first may ultimately choose a life sentence, and vice versa.

The second lacking procedure was the knowledge necessary to determine punishment. The participants were introduced to only a part of the criminal codes related to the case and were not provided with precedent cases. Finally, the audio recordings used as study material omitted important parts of the trial, such as witness testimony, psychiatric examinations, and victim impact statements. Incorporating these essential trial procedures into future research will enhance our understanding of the death penalty decision-making process and will offer useful findings to courts.

Despite the aforementioned issues, our study clearly demonstrates that the decision to choose the death penalty involves a different process than the decision to choose other forms of punishment. This has important implications for future psychological and juristic research on capital punishment.

REFERENCES

Allen, M., Mabry, E., & McKelton, D. M. (1998). Impact of juror attitudes about the death penalty on juror evaluations of guilt and punishment. *Law and Human Behavior, 22*(6), 715-731.

Amnesty International. *Amnesty International Report 2012*. Retrieved from http://www.amnesty.org/en/death-penalty/abolitionist-and-retentionist-countries.

Baker, D. N., Lambert, E. G., & Jenkins, M. (2005). Racial Differences in Death Penalty Support and Opposition A Preliminary Study of White and Black College Students. *Journal of Black Studies, 35*(4), 201-224.

Baumer, E. P., Messner, S. F., & Rosenfeld, R. (2003). Explaining Spatial Variation in Support for Capital Punishment: A Multilevel Analysis1. *American Journal of Sociology, 108*(4), 844-875.

Beckham, C. M., Spray, B. J., & Pietz, C. A. (2007). Jurors' locus of control and defendants' attractiveness in death penalty sentencing. *The Journal of social psychology, 147*(3), 285-298.

Bohm, R. M. (2003). American death penalty opinion: Past, present, and future. In J. R. Acker, R. W. Bohm, & C. S. Lanier (Eds.), *America's experiment with capital punishment: Reflections on the past, present, and future of the ultimate penal sanction* (pp. 27-54). Durham, NC: Carolina Academic Press.

Cabinet Office, Government of Japan. http://www8.cao.go.jp/survey/h21/h21-houseido/2-2.html.

Carlsmith, K. M. (2006). The roles of retribution and utility in determining punishment. *Journal of Experimental Social Psychology, 42*(4), 437–451.

Carlsmith, K. M., Darley, J. M., & Robinson, P. H. (2002). Why do we punish? Deterrence and just deserts as motives for punishment. *Journal of Personality and Social Psychology, 83*, 284-299.

Costanzo, S., & Costanzo, M. (1994). Life or death decisions: An analysis of capital jury decision making under the special issues sentencing framework. *Law and Human Behavior, 18*(2), 151.

Darley, J. M., Carlsmith, K. M., & Robinson, P. H. (2000). Incapacitation and just deserts as motives for punishment. *Law and Human Behavior, 24*(6), 659-683.

Fitzgerald, R., & Ellsworth, P. C. (1984). Due process vs. crime control: Death qualification and jury attitudes. *Law and Human Behavior, 8*(1-2), 31.

Forsterlee, L., Horowitz, I. A., Forsterlee, R., King, K., & Ronlund, L. (1999). Death penalty attitudes and juror decisions in Australia. *Australian Psychologist, 34*(1), 64-69.

Fox, J. A., Radelet, M. L., & Bonsteel, J. L. (1990). Death penalty opinion in the post-Furman years. *NYU Rev. L. & Soc. Change, 18*, 499.

Haidt, J. (2001). The emotional dog and its rational tail: A social intuitionist approach to moral judgment. *Psychology Review, 108*(4), 814-834.

Hessing, D. J., de Keijser, J. W., & Elffers, H. (2003). Explaining Capital Punishment Support in an Abolitionist Country. *Law and Human Behavior, 27*(6), 605-622.

Jacobs, D., & Carmichael, J. T. (2004). Ideology, social threat, and the death sentence: Capital sentences across time and space. *Social Forces, 83*(1), 249-278.

Jacobs, D., Carmichael, J. T., & Kent, S. L. (2005). Vigilantism, current racial threat, and death sentences. *American Sociological Review, 70*(4), 656-677.

Jones, M. B., & Wiener, R. L. (2011). Effects of Mortality Salience on Capital Punishment Sentencing Decisions. *Basic and Applied Social Psychology, 33*(2), 167-181.

Keller, L. B., Oswald, M. E. & Stucki, I. (2010). A closer look at an eye for an eye: Laypersons' punishment decisions are primarily driven by retributive motives. *Social Justice Research, 23*(2-3), 99-116.

Lester, D., Maggioncalda-Aretz, M., & Stark, S. H. (1997). Adolescents' attitudes toward the death penalty. *Adolescence, 32*(126), 447.

Lynch, M., & Haney, C. (2009). Capital jury deliberation: Effects on death sentencing, comprehension, and discrimination. *Law and human behavior, 33*(6), 481-496.

McCann, S. J. (2008). Societal threat, authoritarianism, conservatism, and U.S. state death penalty sentencing (1977-2004). *Journal of personality and social psychology, 94*(5), 913.

Maggard, S. R., Payne, B.K., Chappell, A. T. (2012). Attitudes toward capital punishment: Educational, demographic, and neighborhood crime influences. *The Social Science Journal, 49*(2), 155-166.

Miller, A. S. (1998). Why Japanese religions look different: The social role of religious organizations in Japan. *Review of Religious Research*, 360-370.

Miller, M. K., & Hayward, R. D. (2008). Religious characteristics and the death penalty. *Law and Human Behavior, 32*(2), 113-123.

Mitchell, T. L., Haw, R. M., Pfeifer, J. E., & Meissner, C. A. (2005). Racial Bias in Mock Juror Decision-Making. *Law and Human Behavior, 29*(6), 621-637.

O'Neil, K. M., Patry, M. W., & Penrod, S. D. (2004). Exploring the effects of attitudes toward the death penalty on capital sentencing verdicts. *Psychology, Public Policy, and Law, 10*(4), 443.

Platania, J., & Moran, G. (1999). Due process and the death penalty: The role of prosecutorial misconduct in closing argument in capital trials. *Law and Human Behavior, 23*(4), 471-486.

Poulson, R. L., Braithwaite, R. L., Brondino, M. J., & Wuensch, K. L. (1997). Mock jurors' insanity defense verdict selections: The role of evidence, attitudes, and verdict options. *Journal of Social Behavior and personality, 12*(3), 743-758.

Rucker, D. D., Polifroni, M., Tetlock, P. E., & Scott, A. L. (2004). On the assignment of punishment: The impact of general societal threat and the moderating role of severity. *Personality and Social Psychology Bulletin, 30*(6), 673–684.

Sandys, M., & McGarrell, E. F. (1995). Attitudes toward capital punishment: Preference for the penalty or mere acceptance?. *Journal of Research in Crime and Delinquency, 32*(2), 191-213.

Sporer, S. L., & Goodman-Delahunty, J. (2009). Disparities in sentencing decisions. *Social psychology of punishment of crime*.

Stack, S. (2000). Support for the death penalty: A gender-specific model. *Sex Roles, 43*(3-4), 163-179.

SunWolf. (2007). Facilitating death talk: Creating collaborative courtroom conversations about the death penalty between attorneys and jurors. In L. R. Frey & K. Carragee (Eds.), *Communication activism* (Vol. 1, pp. 273-309). Cresskill, NJ: Hampton Press.

Thompson, W. C., Cowan, C. L., Ellsworth, P. C., & Harrington, J. C. (1984). Death penalty attitudes and conviction proneness: The translation of attitudes into verdicts. *Law and Human Behavior, 8*(1-2), 95.

UNDOC Homicide statistics 2012. Retrieved from http://www.unodc.org /unodc/en/data-and-analysis/homicide.html.

Unnever, J. D., & Cullen, F. T. (2007). The racial divide in support for the death penalty: Does white racism matter?. *Social Forces*, *85*(3), 1281-1301.

Unnever, J. D., & Cullen, F. T. (2010). racial–ethnic intolerance and support for capital punishment: a cross[7] national comparison. *Criminology*, *48*(3), 831-864.

Valliant, P. M., & Oliver, C. L. (1997). Attitudes toward capital punishment: A function of leadership style, gender and personality. *Social Behavior and Personality: an international journal*, *25*(2), 161-168.

Watamura, E., Wakebe, T., Takano, Y. (2010). Lay judges' strategy for determining appropriate sentence: Is it retribution, prevention against a subsequent crime by the offender, or warning for future crimes? *Japanese Journal of Law and Psychology*, *9*(1), 98-108.

Watson, P. J., Ross, D. F., & Morris, R. J. (2003). Borderline personality traits correlate with death penalty decisions. *Personality and individual differences*, *35*(2), 421-429.

Whitehead, J. T., & Blankenship, M. B. (2000). The gender gap in capital punishment attitudes: An analysis of support and opposition. *American Journal of Criminal Justice*, *25*(1), 1-13.

In: Psychology of Punishment
Editor: Nicolas Castro

ISBN: 978-1-62948-103-6
© 2013 Nova Science Publishers, Inc.

Chapter 3

PUNISHMENT AVOIDANCE AND INTENTIONAL RISKY DRIVING BEHAVIOUR: WHAT ARE THE IMPLICATIONS FOR 'GETTING AWAY WITH IT'?

Bridie Scott-Parker[1,2,3], Barry Watson[2,3], Mark J. King[2,3] and Melissa K. Hyde[4,5]

[1]University of the Sunshine Coast Accident Research (USCAR), Faculty of Arts & Business, University of the Sunshine Coast (USC);
[2]Centre for Accident Research & Road Safety – Queensland (CARRS-Q), Queensland University of Technology (QUT);
[3]Institute of Health & Biomedical Innovation (IHBI), QUT;
[4]School of Psychology & Counselling, QUT;
[5]Behavioural Basis of Health, Griffith Health Institute, Griffith University

ABSTRACT

Every motorised jurisdiction mandates legal driving behaviour which facilitates driver mobility and road user safety through explicit road rules that are enforced by regulatory authorities such as the Police. In road safety, traffic law enforcement has been very successfully applied to modify road user behaviour, and increasingly technology is fundamental in detecting illegal road user behaviour. Furthermore, there is also sound evidence that highly visible and/or intensive enforcement programs achieve long-term deterrent effects. To illustrate, in Australia random breath testing has considerably reduced the incidence and prevalence of driving whilst under the influence of alcohol.

There is, however, evidence that many road rules continue to be broken, including speeding and using a mobile phone whilst driving, and there are many instances where drivers are not detected or sufficiently sanctioned for these transgressions. Furthermore, there is a growing body of evidence suggesting that experiences of punishment avoidance – that is, successful attempts at avoiding punishment such as drivers talking themselves out of a ticket, or changing driving routes to evade detection – are associated with and predictive of the extent of illegal driving behaviour and future illegal driving intentions. Therefore there is a need to better understand the phenomenon of punishment avoidance to enhance our traffic law enforcement procedures and therefore safety of all road users.

This chapter begins with a review of the young driver road safety problem, followed by an examination of contemporary deterrence theory to enhance our understanding of both the experiences and implications of punishment avoidance in the road environment. It is noteworthy that in situations where detection and punishment remain relatively rare, such as on extensive road networks, the research evidence suggests that experiences of punishment avoidance may have a stronger influence upon risky driving behaviour than experiences of punishment. Finally, data from a case study examining the risky behaviour of young drivers will be presented, and the implications for 'getting away with it' will be discussed.

INTRODUCTION

Young Driver Road Safety

*"Road crashes are a global epidemic,
a preventable plague on the young."*
(MRS, 2013, p. 21)

Approximately 1.24 million people are fatally injured in road traffic crashes each year around the world, whilst a further 20-50 million people sustain non-fatal injuries. Road traffic crashes are the leading cause of death for young people aged 15-29 years (WHO, 2013). Young drivers aged 17-24 years have been a major public health concern for decades due to their overrepresentation in crash fatality and injury statistics. To illustrate further in the context of the state of Queensland, Australia, persons aged 17-24 years comprise approximately 10.8% of the population (ABS, 2012), however these road users contributed 22.9% of the fatalities in the year to 23 June 2013 (TMR, 2013a). Such road crash statistics arise from a combination primarily of factors pertaining to psychosocial development, deliberate risk taking behaviour, and driving inexperience. In response, motorised jurisdictions have implemented a variety of interventions and countermeasures including driver education and training, media campaigns, in-car technology, incentive programs, peer and parent support programs, legislation, and enforcement programs.

Legislation has been pivotal in the safety of all road users (e.g., seat belt laws in Australia, Milne, 1985; Elliott, 1992; blood alcohol concentration laws, Fell &Voas, 2006; McCartt et al., 2009; Shults et al., 2001; Zwerling & Jones, 1999). One form of legislation specifically targeting young drivers – graduated driver licensing (GDL) – has emerged as particularly effective (e.g., Fell et al., 2011; Karaca-Mandic & Ridgeway, 2010; Lewis-Evans, 2010). GDL is characterised by a multi-stage program which allows the young driver to develop driving and associated skills (such as hazard perception and situation awareness skills) in conditions of reduced risk over an extended period of time. In July 2007, Queensland, Australia, considerably enhanced its GDL program. As can be seen in Figure 1, this GDL program incorporates various conditions, restrictions, and mandatory tests, culminating in an unrestricted Open licence. Importantly, GDL restrictions and conditions for young drivers operate in conjunction with general road rules which must be obeyed by all drivers, such as complying with posted speed limits and not using handheld mobile phones (see TMR, 2013b).

Frequently the efficacy of legislation is dependent upon the acceptance, and therefore the voluntary compliance, of the driving public (Foss et al., 2001; Huq et al., 2011; McCartt & Eichelberger, 2011). Most drivers recognise the importance and purpose of the driving legislation and support its implementation (Mitchell-Taverner et al., 2003). Interestingly, and somewhat perplexingly, compliance with GDL legislation has primarily relied upon the vigilance and efforts of the young driver's parents (e.g., Simons-Morton, 2007; Williams, 2006) in addition to the voluntary compliance of the young driver. Perhaps unsurprisingly then, less compliance with GDL requirements is reported by young drivers who do not support GDL conditions, and less compliance with GDL requirements is reported by young drivers who state that their parents do not support GDL conditions (e.g., Foss & Goodwin, 2003; Goodwin et al., 2006; Williams et al., 2002).

Learner Theory Test

- 16 years minimum age

⇩

Learner Licence

- 1 year minimum duration
- 100 hours of logbook-certified driving practice (10 hours at night; 3 hours credit for 1 hour of professional instruction up to maximum credit of 30 hours)
- Various restrictions (eg, zero blood alcohol concentration, drivers not to use hands-free mobile phones and passengers not to use loudspeaker modes)

⇩

Practical Driving Assessment

⇩

Provisional 1 (P1) licence

- 1 year minimum duration
- Various restrictions (eg, late night passenger restriction, no audible cell phone use in vehicle)

⇩

Hazard Perception Test

⇩

Provisional 2 (P2) licence

- 2 year duration if P1 issued to driver < 23 years and now < 25 years
- 1 year duration if P1 issued to driver < 23 years and now aged ≥ 25 years
- 1 year duration if P1 issued to driver = 23 years and driver now ≥ 24 years
- Various restrictions (eg, high powered vehicle restriction, display novice plates on vehicle)

⇩

Open licence

- Automatic progression from P2 to Open licence
- No restrictions

Figure 1. The graduated driver licensing program introduced in Queensland, Australia, in July 2007.

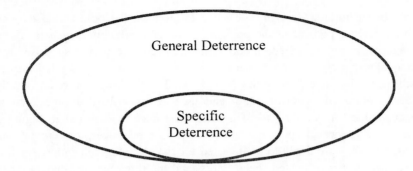

Figure 2. General and specific deterrence.

Legislation, however, is only one part of the equation – *enforcement* of legislation (Travis, 2005) has been and continues to be essential (Williams, 2006; Wundersitz et al., 2010; Yannis et al., 2007; see also Bates et al., 2012). As noted above, laws addressing blood alcohol concentration in particular are highly effective, and enforcement in the form of roadside checks for drink driving not only reduce the rate of alcohol-involved crashes, but all crashes (Erke et al., 2009). Moreover, a lack of enforcement is associated with more risky driving behaviour generally, including driving in excess of posted speed limits, after drinking alcohol, and without wearing a seatbelt (Stanojevic et al., 2013). Indeed drivers of all ages were found to increase their driving speed in response to a decreased risk of detection and apprehension after a 35% reduction in the number of state troopers in Oregon (Bushway et al., 2013). The effects of enforcement, however, do not rely as much on *detection* of offenders as on *deterrence*, and enforcement of road safety legislation, including GDL, is largely premised upon classical deterrence theory.

Deterrence: Theoretical Perspectives and the Experience of Punishment Avoidance

Deterrence theory asserts that a combination of the perceived risk of detection for risky and illegal behaviour, and the swiftness, certainty and severity of punishment for the behaviour, are central to the enforcement's capacity to regulate the risky and illegal behaviour (see Homel, 1988). *Specific* deterrence arises from being apprehended and punished for a risky behaviour, such as driving in excess of posted speed limits: being apprehended and punished for speeding is expected to deter the young driver from speeding again in the future. *General* deterrence arises from the observation of other drivers being apprehended and punished for a risky behaviour, such as driving in excess of posted speed limits. General deterrence may also arise from personal experience of enforcement activities for risky driving behaviours, such as driving at or below the posted speed limit through a point-to-point speed camera enforcement zone, and as such specific deterrence can be conceptualised as an element of general deterrence as depicted in Figure 2. Accordingly, through personal and vicarious experiences, drivers become aware that they are likely to be detected for risky driving behaviours, such as driving in excess of posted speed limits, and the threat of punishment deters them from speeding in their everyday driving (Homel, 1988). The certainty of punishment appears particularly influential. For example in the young driver context, a high certainty of punishment has been found to be associated with less drink driving behaviour (Grosvenor et al., 1999).

A simplistic view of general deterrence implies that there is an ideal situation in which everybody complies because they are deterred by the possibility of detection. In reality, offences will occur, and detection may or may not result. Notwithstanding that the effects of enforcement rely upon deterrence, the driver will not be deterred if their own, or others, risky driving is *not detected*, because apprehension and punishment first require detection. As such, detection is an important element of enforcement activities. Accordingly, Stafford and Warr (1993) argue that deterrence theory does not go far enough to explain the complex interrelationships amongst actions and consequences and the implications for future behaviours. They argue that, following a risky and illegal behaviour, "offenders will always experience punishment or punishment avoidance, and it is dubious to argue that only the former affects subsequent behaviours." (p. 28). Punishment avoidance can be achieved through a multitude of experiences. In the driving context these experiences include the driver changing their driving routes to avoid on-road Police presence (thereby evading detection in the first instance), the driver talking themselves out of a ticket when they have been detected offending, and the driver having someone else 'take the punishment' (such as monetary fines and licence demerit points) for them (in the instance that the offence was photographed and the infringement notice and associated monetary fines and demerit points are notified via mail correspondence).

Punishment avoidance has been found to influence risky driving behaviour (e.g., drink driving, Freeman & Watson, 2006; drug driving, Watling et al., 2010; unlicensed driving, Watson, 2004; and speeding, Fleiter et al., 2006; Fleiter & Watson, 2007); including experiences of vicarious punishment avoidance (e.g., Watling et al., 2010). Perhaps most importantly, punishment avoidance likely reduces the certainty of punishment (Piquero & Pogarsky, 2002; Watling et al., 2010), one of the most important mechanisms underpinning the success of both specific and general deterrence. Problematic for the effective intervention in risky and illegal behaviours in general – rather than being restricted to risky and illegal driving behaviours specifically – is that experiences of punishment avoidance and reward are processed by the same part of the brain (the medial orbitofrontal cortex), meaning that rewards and punishment avoidance are perceived in the same way by the individual (Kim et al., 2006). It is reasonable to conclude at a neurobiological level that each consequence – punishment avoidance or reward – will therefore exert the same influence upon the respective behaviour(s).

This neurobiological finding has considerable implications for safe road use and effective and efficient intervention in road safety in general, and road safety for young drivers specifically. At the most basic level, rewards and punishments are pivotal in the learning, repetition, and cessation of behaviour including risky driving (Beck, 1990), therefore driving behaviour is constantly altered by its consequences (Fuller, 2002). Rewards are motivating, acting as incentives to gain expected outcomes, and are reinforcing. Anticipated driving rewards such as a faster journey, motivate and reinforce risky behaviours such as speeding, thereby increasing the likelihood the young driver speeds in the future. In contrast, punishments serve to prevent, curtail, or extinguish learned behaviours. Consistent with deterrence theory, the young driver who is detected speeding and receives a fine and demerit points is less likely to speed in similar circumstances in the future. However, as noted earlier the effect of punishment avoidance is akin to rewards, and consequentially, risky driving behaviour is rewarded (albeit inadvertently) when there is no punishment. Moreover, having personally or vicariously experienced punishment avoidance, the young driver may change their future driving journeys to maximise the likelihood that they can continue to avoid punishment.

Furthermore, Police are central as the primary enforcers of GDL and general road rule legislation in motorised jurisdictions. Frequently Police have discretionary authority in enforcing legislation. Research has indicated that Police with a shorter service history and who believed laws were excessive for young drinking drivers were more likely to use discretion and thus not issue citations to young drivers detected drink driving (Meyers et al., 1989), allowing the young driver to avoid punishment for their risky and illegal driving behaviours. The nature and bounds of Police discretionary authority have legal bases that no doubt vary by jurisdiction, and policy and practice constraints that may change from time to time and by location within jurisdictions. It is rare to find official information about the scope of Police discretion in any particular jurisdiction, and even less common to find reliable information about how this is translated into practice. This means that much remains unknown about the impact of Police discretion to not apprehend and punish offenders. Nor do we fully understand the synergies of Police discretion, punishment avoidance, and subsequent risky driving behaviour of drivers of all ages. In addition, much remains unknown about the driver's experiences of punishment avoidance, whether directly through such mechanisms as Police discretion, and indirectly by, for example, deliberately choosing to change their driving route to avoid on-road Police presence.

Punishment Avoidance and the Young Driver

The role of punishment avoidance in the risky behaviour of young drivers was first highlighted in the qualitative research of Scott-Parker et al. (2012a). Small group and individual discussions with 21 young drivers regarding the influence of Police on young driver risky behaviour revealed that some young drivers had experienced a lack of punishment by Police for risky driving. Punishment-avoidant behaviour included receiving an informal warning for risky driving behaviours, and talking their way out of ticket, at the time they were pulled over to the side of the road. In addition, young drivers reported that on occasion the Police officer failed to detect simultaneous offences at the time of apprehension, including GDL-specific offences such as violating night-time passenger limits. Interestingly the behaviours and punitive actions of the Police were also seen to depend upon a variety of factors, including the reaction of the young driver at the time they were apprehended.

Young drivers also reported that they deliberately avoided areas of known Police presence, thereby ensuring that they could not be detected nor apprehended for risky and illegal driving behaviours, and as such they had successfully avoided anticipated punishment for risky and illegal driving behaviours. Such experiences of punishment avoidance – ranging from changing driving routes to talking themselves out of a ticket – were reported to be influential in the young driver's subsequent driving. In particular, young drivers reported deliberate route changes and information sharing regarding on-road Police presence, with young male drivers advising that they viewed the Police with disdain and felt that the Police unfairly persecuted them due to their age and driving inexperience in particular. Most importantly for road safety and effective intervention, the young driver perceived all forms of punishment avoidance as directly rewarding (Scott-Parker et al., 2012a), therefore the risky driving behaviour(s) undertaken are more likely to be engaged in than extinguished or deterred.

Given the qualitative research findings, the notion of punishment avoidance, including the experience of parents 'taking the punishment' in instances of camera-detected offending, was explored further in a Queensland-wide survey of more than 1200 Learner drivers and a subsample of nearly 400 of these Learners with six months P1 driving experience (2012b). A very small proportion of participants reported that their parents had taken the punishment on their behalf: eight of the Learners (0.8% of the sample) and nine of the P1 drivers (2.7% of the sample). Interestingly, nearly half of the Learners who reported their parents had taken their punishment reported they had been detected for a driving offence during the subsequent 6 months of their P1 driving, whilst the P1 drivers who advised their parents had taken their punishment reported significantly more speeding behaviour.

The punishment avoidance characteristics of the P1 drivers with their own car were also compared to the P1 drivers who did not have their own car 6 months after Provisional licensure. Sixteen percent of these P1 drivers reported avoiding on-road Police presence (25.0% of males and 12.7% of females), with a larger proportion of avoiders reporting an offence (20.9%, compared to 15.8% of non-avoiders). A significantly larger proportion of P1 drivers who had their own car reported they had 'talked their way of a ticket' when detected offending by Police, suggesting that the young driver was highly motivated to avoid receiving an infringement notice or other penalty. In addition, drivers who reported that their parents 'took the punishment' on their behalf reported significantly more driving exposure each week (measured as driving duration), and drivers who reported talking their way out of a ticket at the time of detection also reported significantly greater driving exposure each week (measured as driving distance) (2011). A Queensland-wide survey of 1268 drivers one year after obtaining their P1 licence revealed that a significantly larger proportion of participants who reported driving after drinking alcohol reported avoiding Police (32.0% of drink drivers, 12.6% of non-drink drivers, $p < .01$), and a significantly larger proportion of participants who reported driving after consuming illicit drugs reported avoiding Police (35.0% of drug drivers, 14.7% of non-drug drivers, $p < .001$) (Scott-Parker et al., 2013). These findings are also consistent with the young driver being motivated to avoid detection and punishment.

As can be seen, punishment avoidance appears influential in the risky behaviour of the young driver during the Learner licence phase and during the first 12 months of the P1 licence (2012b, 2013). Accordingly, the Authors examined the influence of punishment avoidance upon the risky behaviour of young drivers with 12 months independent driving experience (on the cusp of advancing from a P1 licence to a P2 licence). The case study below summarises the research and the key findings.

CASE STUDY

Study Aims

The case study aimed (a) to explore the magnitude of punishment avoidance by P1 drivers with 12 month's independent driving experience, and (b) to explore the relationship between punishment avoidance and self-reported risky driving behaviour, including self-reported crashes and offences, and intentions to and the likelihood of bending road rules in future driving. Whilst punishment avoidance conceptually incorporates experiences including the young driver talking themselves out of a ticket at the time of detection, and having their parent(s) take the punishment on their behalf in instances of photographed offences, for the purposes of the case study, punishment avoidance refers to deliberately avoiding the on-road presence of Police and therefore evading the possibility of detection and apprehension for driving-related offences.

Method

Participants
Drivers (n = 1268, 373 males) aged 17-26 years (M =19.09, SD = 2.11) completed a paper survey one year after obtaining their Queensland Provisional 1 (P1) driver's licence (see Figure 1).

Design and Procedure
Every driver in Queensland who progressed from a Learner to a P1 licence in the period April through June 2010 was sent a paper survey by the stategovernment licensing authority (Department of Transport and Main

Roads) on behalf of the research team one year after obtaining their licence. Of the 9393 drivers aged 17 years and older who were eligible to participate, 1268 surveys were returned by drivers aged 17-26 years and were retained for the current research project.

Materials

The paper survey included items exploring driver gender and age; paying attention to (*no, yes*), and avoiding on-road Police presence (*no, yes*) measured through the item "*Do you avoid the areas where you know police are, or are likely to be?*"; future driving intentions to bend[4] road rules (1 *definitely will not*, 7 *definitely will*), and likelihood of bending (1 *very unlikely*, 7 *very likely*) road rules; and self-reported crash involvement and offence detection (*no, yes*). The survey also contained the 44-item Behaviour of Young Novice Drivers Scale (BYNDS) (Scott-Parker et al., 2010) exploring self-reported risky driving behaviour (1 *never*, 5 *nearly all the time*), including driving after drinking alcohol (herein referred to as 'drink driving') and driving after taking illicit drugs such as marijuana and ecstasy (herein referred to as 'drug driving').

Statistical Analysis

Missing data was not imputed; rather, cases were excluded analysis-by-analysis in Statistical Package for the Social Sciences (SPSS) Version 20. Means were compared using analysis of variance and Pearson chi-square, evaluated at significance $\alpha = .05$. Hierarchical multiple regression analyses sample size requirements of ($50+8m$ predictors) for 80% preferred power and .20 medium effect size were met.

Results

One hundred and ninety-three participants (15.2% of the participants; 23.3% of males, 11.9% of females, $p < .001$) reported that they avoided on-road Police presence (herein referred to as *avoiders*). It is reasonable to assert that avoiding on road-Police presence is facilitated by paying attention to on-road Police presence, and consistent with this assertion significantly more

---

[4] Pilot small group interviews conducted by the first author (unpublished, which informed the research of Scott-Parker et al., 2009a, 2009b) explored the perception of road rule transgressions. Young novice drivers reported that 'minor' transgressions such as texting whilst driving were only 'bending' the road rules, whilst in contrast 'major' transgressions such as speeding by 20 kilometres per hour were 'breaking' the road rules. Therefore 'bend' was incorporated in the research to ensure the full novice driving experience was captured.

avoiders reported paying attention to on-road Police presence (95.3% of avoiders paid attention, compared to 90.3% of non-avoiders, $p < .05$).

Overall, 280 participants ($n = 208$, 23.3% of females; $n = 72$, 19.5% of males) reported they had been involved in a car crash in the past 12 months. A larger proportion of avoiders reported being involved in a crash (26.6%) than non-avoiders (21.4%, ns). Consistent with this general finding, a larger proportion of male avoiders (23.3%) than male non-avoiders (18.3%, ns) reported being involved in a crash; and a larger proportion of female avoiders (29.2%) than non-avoiders (22.5%, ns) reported being involved in a crash. Overall, 226 participants ($n = 297$, 33.3% of females; $n = 129$, 34.9% of males) reported being detected for a driving-related offence in the past 12 months. A significantly larger proportion of avoiders reported having an offence detected (42.5%) than non-avoiders (23.6%, $p < .001$). Consistent with this general finding, a significantly larger proportion of male avoiders (51.8%) than male non-avoiders (29.4%, $p < .001$) reported having an offence, and a significantly larger proportion of female avoiders (34.9%) than non-avoiders (21.6%, $p < .01$) having an offence detected in the past 12 months.

Avoiders reported significantly more risky driving behaviour as measured by the BYNDS (avoiders $M = 88.3$, $SD = 15.3$; non-avoiders $M = 76.9$, $SD = 14.2$; $p < .001$). An examination of the individual items within the BYNDS revealed that generally avoiders reported significantly more risky driving behaviour (see Table 1). To further explore the role of avoidance in self-reported risky driving behaviour, a hierarchical multiple regression was conducted with gender and age controlled in the first step, and self-reported police-avoidance entered at the second step. As shown in Table 2, the overall model was significant, explaining just over 8% of variance in self-reported risky driving behaviour, $F(3, 1197) = 35.56$, $p < .001$. In the final model, age and police-avoidance were significant predictors of risky driving, with more risky driving reported by younger drivers and drivers who avoided Police.

Punishment avoiders reported significantly more risky driving intentions (18.1% of avoiders intend to bend road rules in future, compared to 7.2% of non-avoiders, $p < .001$), and greater likelihood of risky driving in the future (33.5% of avoiders likely to bend road rules in future, compared to 24.8% of non-avoiders, $p < .001$). Male drivers also reported significantly more risky future driving intentions (24.1% of male avoiders likely to bend road rules in future, compared to 13.1% of female avoiders, $p < .001$). Similar proportions of male and female avoiders reported a likelihood of being risky (39.0% of male avoiders likely to bend road rules in future, compared to 35.8% of female avoiders, ns) in their future driving.

Table 1. The items within the subscales of the Behaviour of Young Novice Drivers (BYNDS) and their mean and standard deviation for drivers who reported they did and did not engage in punishment avoidance

Item	Punishment avoidance n = 187 M (SD)	No Punishment Avoidance n = 1048 M (SD)
Transient Violations		
You drove over the speed limit in areas where it was unlikely there was a radar or speed camera	2.7 (1.0)	1.9 (1.0)***
You went 10-20 km/hr over the speed limit (eg 72 km/hr in a 60 km/hr zone, 112 km/hr in a 100 km/hr zone)	2.1 (1.0)	1.6 (0.8)***
You deliberately sped when overtaking	2.7 (1.2)	2.1 (1.0)***
You sped at night on roads that were not well lit	1.7 (0.9)	1.3 (0.6)***
You went up to 10 km/hr over the speed limit (eg 65 km/hr in a 60 km/hr zone, 105 km/hr in a 100 km/hr zone)	3.0 (1.0)	2.5 (1.0)***
You went more than 20 km/hr over the speed limit (eg 60 km/hr in 40 km/hr zone, 120 km/hr in 100 km/hr zone)	1.8 (0.8)	1.4 (0.7)***
You raced out of an intersection when the light went green	2.3 (1.1)	1.7 (0.9)***
You travelled in the right lane on multi-lane highways	2.6 (1.2)	2.2 (1.0)***
You sped up when the lights went yellow	2.6 (1.0)	2.2 (1.0)***
You went too fast around a corner	1.8 (0.7)	1.6 (0.7)***
You did an illegal U-turn	1.7 (0.9)	1.4 (0.7)***
You overtook someone on the left	1.9 (1.0)	1.8 (1.0)***
You spoke on a mobile that you held in your hands	1.9 (0.9)	1.5 (0.8)*
Subscale	29.6 (7.8)	22.9(6.8)*
Fixed Violations		
Your passengers didn't wear seatbelts	1.2 (0.6)	1.1 (0.3)***

Table 1. (Continued)

Item	Punishment Avoidance n = 187 M (SD)	No Punishment Avoidance n = 1048 M (SD)
You drove after taking an illicit drug such as marijuana or ecstasy	1.2 (0.6)	1.0 (0.3)***
You carried more passengers than could legally fit in your car	1.1 (0.5)	1.0 (0.2)***
You didn't always wear your seatbelt	1.2 (0.6)	1.1 (0.3)***
You drove without a valid licence as because you hadn't applied for one yet or it had been suspended	1.1 (0.5)	1.0 (0.9)
You didn't wear a seatbelt if it was only for a short trip	1.2 (0.7)	1.1 (0.4)***
If there was no red light camera, you drove through intersections on a red light	1.2 (0.5)	1.1 (0.3)***
You carried more passengers than there were seatbelts for in your car	1.1 (0.4)	1.0 (0.2)***
You drove when you thought you may have been over the legal alcohol limit	1.4 (0.7)	1.1 (0.4)***
You drove a high-powered vehicle	1.2 (0.7)	1.1 (0.4)***
Subscale	11.8 (3.4)	10.6 (1.3)
Misjudgements		
You misjudged the speed when you were exiting a main road	1.6 (0.8)	1.4 (0.6)**
You misjudged the speed of an oncoming vehicle	1.5 (0.7)	1.4 (0.6)**
You misjudged the gap when you were turning right	1.3 (0.7)	1.2 (0.4)***
You misjudged the stopping distance you needed	1.7 (0.7)	1.5 (0.7)***
You turned right into the path of another vehicle	1.2 (0.7)	1.1 (0.4)**
You misjudged the gap when you were overtaking another vehicle	1.4 (0.7)	1.2 (0.5)***
You missed your exit or turn	2.3 (0.9)	2.1 (0.8)*
You entered the road in front of another vehicle	1.8 (0.7)	1.5 (0.6)
You didn't always indicate when you were changing lanes	1.9 (1.1)	1.4 (0.8)

Item	Punishment Avoidance n = 187 M (SD)	No Punishment Avoidance n = 1048 M (SD)
Subscale	12.7 (3.4)	11.2 (2.6)
Risky Exposure		
You drove on the weekend	4.3 (0.8)	4.1 (1.0)**
You drove in the rain	3.3 (0.9)	3.2 (0.8)*
You drove at peak times in the morning and afternoon	3.3 (1.1)	3.3 (1.2)
You drove at night	3.9 (1.0)	3.8 (1.0)
You drove at dusk or dawn	3.7 (1.1)	3.4 (1.2)**
You carried your friends as passengers at night	2.6 (1.1)	2.3 (1.0)***
You drove when you knew you were tired	2.8 (1.1)	2.4 (1.0)***
Your car was full of your friends as passengers	2.6 (1.1)	2.2 (1.1)***
You went for a drive with your mates giving you directions to where they wanted to go	2.6 (1.0)	2.2 (1.0)***
Subscale	28.9 (5.7)	26.8 (5.8)*
Driver Mood		
Your driving was affected by negative emotions like anger or frustration	2.3 (1.1)	1.9 (0.9)***
You allowed your driving style to be influenced by what mood you were in	2.2 (1.0)	1.7 (0.8)***
You drove faster if you were in a bad mood	2.3 (1.0)	1.8 (0.9)***
Subscale	6.8 (2.8)	5.4 (2.3)***

Adapted from Scott-Parker, Watson, & King, 2010.

$* p < .05$, $** p < .01$, $*** p < .001$.

Table 2. Hierarchical multiple regression results for gender, age and punishment avoidance predicting self-reported risky driving behaviour

Variables	β	p	sr^2	R^2	$Adj\ R^2$	ΔR^2
Step One						
Gender	-.03	.231				
Age	-.09	.002	.01			
				.015***	.013	.015
Step Two						
Avoid Police	.26	< .001	.07			
				.082***	.080	.067

*** $p < .001$. Final model is illustrated.

DISCUSSION

This chapter began with an overview of young driver road safety, noting that it is a considerable public health concern. As such effective and efficient intervention is crucial. Legislation and enforcement were identified as two effective mechanisms of intervention, and the underpinning philosophy of deterrence theory was reviewed. Additionally, Stafford and Warr's (1993) reconceptualisation of deterrence theory to incorporate punishment avoidance was discussed, and prior investigation by the Authors of the punishment avoidance phenomena operationalised by young drivers was summarised. Finally, a case study revealed that nearly one-sixth of participants were deliberate avoiders of on-road Police presence, with approximately one quarter of males engaging in this behaviour. Consistent with the reviewed literature, punishment avoiders were more risky drivers in general, reporting more crashes, and significantly more risky driving behaviours (as measured by the BYNDS), offences, and avoiders anticipated riskier driving behaviours in their future journeys.

The literature review and the case study suggest that attempts at punishment avoidance appear to be a considerable influence upon the risky behaviour of young drivers. Indeed, it may be a stronger influence than the actual experience of punishment. As such, two avenues of countermeasure appear to be required. First, there is a need to minimise punishment avoidance opportunities. In this regard, Police are encouraged to utilise random on-road enforcement activities which broadly target all offences (e.g., drivers submitted to a random breath test could also have the validity of their driver's licence and vehicle registration examined and the seatbelt wearing practices of the driver and their passengers examined) and specifically target key offences such as driving in excess of speed limits. Central to avoiding on-road Police presence is the prior or current knowledge of the locations of the on-road Police presence. Accordingly, multiple random and mobile deployment is recommended, particularly to counter young drivers 'paying attention' to, and then avoiding, on-road Police presence.

Second, there is a need to challenge the rewards associated with and inherent within punishment avoidance, particularly for young drivers embarking on their driving careers. A reduction in opportunities to avoid on-road Police presence will assist, as will efforts that ensure that the correct person is punished where automated enforcement is utilised (such as with speed and/or red light camera detection). Moreover, further research is required to elucidate the nature of punishment-avoidant interactions, particularly leniency (Schafer & Mastrofski, 2005), between Police and young drivers (including talking-themselves-out-of-tickets and missed consecutive offences) to minimise the likelihood that risky behaviour will be repeated by the young driver. Moreover, the considerable dearth of research examining both the nature and impact of Police discretion more generally requires investigation.

Notwithstanding study limitations, such as a low response rate in the Queensland-wide case study (approximately 14.4% of drivers of all ages eligible to participate in the research completed a survey, however the response rate of young drivers only was unable to be determined), and a reliance on self-report including crash and offence data, the research findings provide important insight into the risky behaviours of young drivers, and in particular the risky behaviour of young drivers who actively engage in punishment avoidance. The persistence of risky behaviour even after personal experience of deterrence measures such as infringement notices – evidenced by the continued risky behaviour of case-study avoiders who had previously been detected offending – suggests that researchers should consider other psychosocial factors that have been found to influence the risky behaviour of the young novice driver (Lonero & Clinton, 1998). As such, the influence of factors such as attitudes (e.g., Sarma et al., 2013), sensation seeking propensity (see Jonah, 1997, for a review), riskiness of friends (e.g., Simons-Morton et al., 2012), and parental modelling of risky driving behaviour (e.g., Taubman-Ben-Ari et al., 2005) upon punishment avoidance requires further examination. Furthermore, prior research, such as the finding that male young drivers who are detected for a speeding offence are twice as likely to again be detected for a speeding offence compared to those who had not been detected for a speeding offence (Lawpoolsri et al., 007), suggests that enforcement alone is not sufficient to effect behaviour change in young drivers (Zaal, 1994). This appears to be the case for young drivers who have experienced and continue to experience punishment avoidance deliberately through their driving behaviours and inadvertently through personal interactions with Police (in the instance of on-road enforcement) and via distal interactions with enforcement authorities (in the instance of automated enforcement).

CONCLUSION

Young driver road safety has been and continues to be of great concern to road safety researchers, practitioners and policy-makers around the world. The combination of legislation and enforcement is one of the most effective interventions applied to date. Legislation and enforcement are underpinned by the philosophy of deterrence which includes the personal and vicarious experience of punishment as its foundation. Punishment can only eventuate after detection, and punishment avoidance efforts such as deliberately changing driving routes to avoid on-road Police presence mean that driving offences cannot be detected, let alone punished. Therefore it appears that rather than the experience of punishment as the champion of behaviour change, regulating and preventing all drivers – and young drivers in particular – from engaging in risky and illegal driving behaviours, punishment avoidance undermines the general and specific benefits afforded by community policing. In a case study, young drivers who reported that they actively avoided on-road Police presence, thereby avoiding any chance of being punished for risky and illegal driving behaviours, reported the most risky driving behaviour and anticipated more risky driving in the future. Further research is required to investigate the nature and impact of Police discretion in particular, and efforts need to minimise punishment avoidance opportunities for young drivers whilst reducing the rewards received for punishment avoidance behaviours.

ACKNOWLEDGMENTS

Special thanks to the Queensland Department of Transport and Main Roads (formerly Queensland Transport) for their assistance in the recruitment of novice drivers for the case study. The first author was the recipient of a National Health and Medical Research Council Postgraduate Research Scholarship at the time of data collection.

REFERENCES

ABS. (2012). *2011 Census QuickStats Queensland.* Australian Bureau of Statistics. Retrieved 1 March 2013 from http://www.censusdata. abs.gov.au/census_services/getproduct/census/2011/quickstat/3

Bates, L., Soole, D. & Watson, B. (2012). The effectiveness of traffic policing in reducing traffic crashes. In Prenzler, Tim (Ed.), *Policing and Security in Practice: Challenges and Achievements.* Palgrave Macmillan, United Kingdom, 90-109.

Beck, R. C. (1990). *Motivation: Theories and principles* (3rd ed.). New Jersey: Prentice-Hall.

Bushway, S., DeAngelo, G. & Hansen, B. (2013). Deterability by age. *International Review of Law and Economics.*

Elliott, B. (1992). *Achieving high levels of compliance with road safety laws: A review of road user behaviour modification.* Brisbane: Queensland Parliamentary Travelsafe Committee.

Erke, A., Goldenbeld, C. & Vaa, T. (2009). The effects of drink-driving checkpoints on crashes – A meta-analysis. *Accident Analysis and Prevention, 41,* 914-923.

Fell, J. C., Jones, K., Romano, E. & Voas, R. (2011). An evaluation of graduated driver licensing effects on fatal crash involvements of young drivers in the United States. *Traffic Injury Prevention, 12*(5), 423-431.

Fell, J. C. & Voas, R. B. (2006). The effectiveness of reducing illegal blood alcohol concentration (BAC) limits for driving: Evidence for lowering the limit to .05 BAC. *Journal of Safety Research, 37,* 233-243.

Fleiter, J. J., Lennon, A. & Watson, B. (2007). Choosing not to speed: A qualitative exploration of differences in perceptions about speed limit compliance and related issues. Paper presented at the *Australasian Road Safety Research Policing Education Conference*, Melbourne, 17-19 October. Melbourne.

Fleiter, J. J. & Watson, B. (2006). The speed paradox: the misalignment between driver attitudes and speeding behaviour. *Journal of the Australasian College of Road Safety, 17*(2), 23-30.

Freeman, J. E. & Watson, B. C. (2006). An application of Stafford and Warr's reconceptualization of deterrence*Accident Analysis and Prevention, 38,* 462-471.

Foss, R. & Goodwin, A. (2003). Enhancing the effectiveness of graduated driver licensing legislation. *Journal of Safety Research, 34,* 79-84.

Foss, R. D., Stewart, J. R. & Reinfurt, D. W. (2001). Evaluation of the effects of North Carolina's 0.08% BAC law. *Accident Analysis and Prevention, 33,* 507-517.

Fuller, R. (2002). The psychology of the young driver. In R. Fuller, and J. A. Santos (Eds.), *Human factors for highway engineers* (241-253). Oxford: Elsevier.

Goodwin, A. H., Wells, J. K., Foss, R. D. & Williams, A. F. (2006). Encouraging compliance with graduated driver licensing restrictions. *Journal of Safety Research, 37,* 343-351.

Grosvenor, D., Toomey, T. L. & Wagenaar, A. C. (1999). Deterrence and the adolescent drinking driver. *Journal of Safety Research, 30,* 187-191.

Homel, R. (1988). *Policing and punishing the drinking driver: A study of general and specific deterrence.* New York: Springer-Verlag.

Huq, A., Tyler, T. R. & Schulhofer, S. J. (2011). Why does the public cooperate with law enforcement? The influence of the purposes and targets of policing. *Psychology, Public Policy, and Law, August,* 419-450.

Jonah, B. A. (1997). Sensation seeking and risky driving: A review and synthesis of the literature. *Accident Analysis and Prevention, 29,* 651-665.

Karaca-Mandic, P. & Ridgeway, G. (2010). Behavioral impact of graduated driver licensing on teenage driving risk and exposure. *Journal of Health Economics, 29*(1), 48-61.

Kim, H., Shimojo, S., O'Doherty, J. P. (2006). Is avoiding an aversive outcome rewarding? Neural substrates of avoidance learning in the human brain. *PLOS One.* Retrieved 1 March 2013 from http://www.plosbiology. org/article/info%3Adoi%2F10.1371%2Fjournal.pbio.0040233

Lawpoolsri, S., Li, J. & Braver, E. R. (2007). Do speeding tickets reduce the likelihood of receiving subsequent speeding tickets? A longitudinal study of speeding violators in Maryland. *Traffic Injury Prevention, 8,* 26-34.

Lewis-Evans, B. (2010). Crash involvement during the different phases of the New Zealand graduated driver licensing system (GDLS). *Journal of Safety Research, 41,* 359-365.

Lonero, L. P. & Clinton, K. M. (1998). *Changing road user behaviour: What works and what doesn't.* Toronto: PDE Publications.

McCartt, A. T. & Eichelberger, A. (2011). *Attitudes toward red light camera enforcement in cities with camera programs.* Arlington: Insurance Institute for Highway Safety.

McCartt, A. T., Hellinga, L. A. & Kirley, B. B. (2009). Effects of 21 minimum legal drinking age laws on alcohol-related driving in the United States. Young impaired drivers. *The nature of the problem and possible solutions.* Transportation Research Circular Number E-C132, 124-139. Washington: TRB.

Meyers, A. R., Heeren, T. & Hingson, R. (1989). Discretionary leniency in police enforcement of laws against drinking and driving: Two examples from the state of Maine, USA. *Journal of Criminal Justice, 17,* 179-186.

Milne, P. W. (1985*). Fitting and wearing of seat belts in Australia. The history of a successful countermeasure.* Canberra: AGPS.

Mitchell-Taverner, P., Zipparo, L. & Goldsworthy, J. (2003). *Survey on speeding and enforcement. CR 214a.* Canberra: ATSB.

MRS. (2013). *Make roads safe for all.* Make Roads Safe. Retrieved 1 March 2013 from http://www.makeroadssafe.org/Documents/mrs_safe_roads_for_all.pdf

Piquero, A. R. & Pogarsky, G. (2002). Beyond Stafford and Warr's reconceptualization of deterrence: Personal and vicarious experiences, impulsivity, and offending behavior. *Journal of Research in Crime and Delinquency, 39,* 153-186.

Sarma, K. M., Carey, R. N., Kervick, A. A. & Bimpeh, Y. (2013). Psychological factors associated with indices of risky, reckless and cautious driving in a national sample of drivers in the Republic of Ireland. *Accident Analysis and Prevention, 50,* 1226-1235.

Schafer, J. A. & Mastrofski, S. D. (2005). Police leniency in traffic enforcement encounters: Exploratory findings from observations and interviews. *Journal of Criminal Justice, 33,* 225-238.

Scott-Parker, B., Watson, B. & King, M. J. (2009a). Understanding the psychosocial factors influencing the risky behaviour of young drivers. *Transportation Research Part F: Traffic Psychology and Behaviour, 12,* 470-482.

Scott-Parker, B., Watson, B., King, M. J. (2009b). Exploring how parents and peers influence the behaviour of young drivers. *2009 Australasian Road Safety Research, Policing and Education Conference,* 10-12 November, 2009, Sydney, New South Wales, Australia.

Scott-Parker, B., Watson, B. & King, M. J. (2010). The risky behaviour of young drivers: Developing a measurement tool. *Proceedings of the 24th*

Canadian Multidisciplinary Road Safety Conference, Niagara Falls, Canada, June 6-9, 2010.

Scott-Parker, B., Watson, B., King, M. J. & Hyde, M. K. (2011). Mileage, car ownership, experience of punishment avoidance and the risky driving of young drivers. *Traffic Injury Prevention, 12*(6), 559-567.

Scott-Parker, B., Watson, B., King, M. J. & Hyde, M. K. (2012a). "They're lunatics on the road": Exploring the normative influences of parents, friends, and police on young novice's risky driving decisions. *Safety Science, 50*, 1917-1928.

Scott-Parker, B., Watson, B., King, M. J. & Hyde, M. K. (2012b). Young, inexperienced and on the road – Do novice drivers comply with road rules? *Transportation Research Record: Journal of the Transportation Research Board of the National Academies,* No. 2318, Transportation Research Board of the National Academies, Washington, D.C., 2012, 98–106.

Scott-Parker, B., Watson, B., King, M. J. & Hyde, M. K. (2013). "I drove after drinking alcohol" and other risky driving behaviours reported by young novice drivers. In conference proceedings of *International Council on Alcohol, Drugs, and Traffic Safety Conference*, August 2013.

Shults, R., Elder, R. W., Sleet, D. A., Nichols, J., L., Alao, M. O., Carande-Kulis, V., G.,...the Task Force on Community Preventive Services. (2001). Reviews of evidence regarding interventions to reduce alcohol-impaired driving. *American Journal of Preventive Medicine, 21*(4S), 66-88.

Simons-Morton, B. (2007). Parent involvement in novice teen driving: Rationale, evidence of effects, and potential for enhancing graduated driver licensing effectiveness. *Journal of Safety Research, 38*, 193-202.

Simons-Morton, B., Ouimet, M. C., Chen, R., Klauer, S., Lee, S. L., Wang, J., Dingus, T. A. (2012). Peer influence predicts speeding prevalence among teenage drivers. *Journal of Safety Research, 43*, 397-403.

Stafford, M. C. & Warr, M. (1993). A reconceptualization of general and specific deterrence. *Journal of Research in Crime and Delinquency, 30*, 123-125.

Stanojevic, P., Jovanovic, D. & Lajunen, T. (2013). Influence of traffic enforcement on the attitudes and behavior of drivers. *Accident Analysis and Prevention, 52*, 29-38.

Taubman-Ben-Ari, O., Mikulincer, M. & Gillath, O. (2005). From parents to children – Similarity in parents and offspring driving styles. *Transportation Research Part F, 8*, 19-29.

TMR. (2013a). *Queensland Road Toll Report No: 803, Comparative Queensland Road Toll Year to Date to Sunday, 23 June 2013*. Transport and Main Roads. Retrieved 24 June 2013 from http://www.tmr.qld.gov. au/Safety/Transport-and-road-statistics/Road-safety-statistics.aspx

TMR. (2013b). Queensland road rules. Transport and Main Roads. Retrieved 1 March 2013 from http://www.tmr.qld.gov.au/safety/queensland-road-rules.aspx

Travis, L. E. (2005). *Introduction to criminal justice* (5th ed.). Matthew Bender & Co: Cincinnati.

Watling, C., Freeman, J., Palk, G. R. & Davey, J. D. (2011). Sex, drugs, and deterrence: Applyng Stafford and Warr's reconceptualization of deterrence theory to drug driving across the genders. In N. M. R. Palmetti, J.P (Ed.), *Psychology of Punishment* (57-71): Nova Science Publishers, Inc.

Watson, B. C. (2004). How effective is deterrence In *Road Safety Research, Policing and Education Conference*, 14 - 16 November, 2004, Perth, Western Australia.

WHO. (2013). Road traffic injuries Fact sheet No. 358, March 2013. World Health Organization. Retrieved 1 March 2013 from http://www.who.int/mediacentre/factsheets/fs358/en/

Williams, A. F. (2006). Parents' views of teen driving risks, the role of parents, and how they plan to manage the risks. *Journal of Safety Research, 37*, 221-226.

Williams, A. F., Nelson, L. A. & Leaf, W. A. (2002). Responses of teenagers and their parents to California's graduated licensing system. *Accident Analysis and Prevention, 34*, 835-842.

Wundersitz, L. N., Doecke, S. D. & Baldock, M. R. J. (2010). *Annual performance indicators of enforced driver behaviours in South Australia, 2008*. CASR Report Series CASR073. Adelaide: CASR.

Yannis, G., Papadimitriou, E. & Antoniou, C. (2007). Impact of enforcement on traffic accidents and fatalities: A multivariate multilevel analysis. *Safety Science, 46*(5), 738-750.

Zaal, D. (1994). *Traffic law enforcement: A review of the literature* (Report number 53). Canberra: Monash University Accident Research Centre.

Zwerling, C. & Jones, M. P. (1999). Evaluation of the effectiveness of low blood alcohol concentration laws for younger drivers. *American Journal of Preventive Medicine, 16*(1), 76-80.

In: Psychology of Punishment   ISBN: 978-1-62948-103-6
Editor: Nicolas Castro   © 2013 Nova Science Publishers, Inc.

Chapter 4

DELAYED PUNISHMENT: AN OVERVIEW AND FUTURE DIRECTIONS

James N. Meindl[*] *and Neal Miller*

The University of Memphis, Memphis, TN, US

ABSTRACT

Years of research on the effective use of punishers has shown that the most effective punishers are those which a) are intense, b) are inescapable, c) occur after every response, d) do not compete against reinforcers, e) are removed and then reintroduced, and f) are delivered immediately following a response. Although these qualities have been shown to increase a punisher's effectiveness, they are often difficult to control outside of laboratory settings. From a clinical perspective, one of the most difficult qualities to control may be the immediate delivery of a punisher, and for a variety of reasons there may be a delay between a response and the delivery of a scheduled punisher. Despite this reality, little recent research has been conducted on strategies to increase the suppressive effect of a delayed punisher. In this chapter we will describe the delay-of-punishment gradient (Kamin, 1959) as well as discuss the implications for the clinical application of punishers. We will review both basic and applied research on the effective use of delayed punishers and highlight applied studies demonstrating behavior suppression with delayed punishers.

[*] Corresponding author: James N. Meindl, Ph. D., BCBA-D, Assistant Professor. The University of Memphis, 400A Ball Hall, Memphis, Tn 38152. E-mail: jnmeindl@memphis.edu.

Finally, we will discuss the importance of conducting further research focused on increasing the suppressive effect of a delayed punisher.

INTRODUCTION

Whenever a person engages in some behavior, whether it be speaking, throwing a ball, writing a paper, or any other myriad possible actions, that behavior inevitably changes the environment such that the conditions present before the emission of the behavior are somehow different than the conditions present after. These environmental changes play a significant role in determining whether that specific behavior will occur more or less frequently in the future. Those changes that increase the future likelihood of behavior are called reinforcers, and those that decrease the future likelihood are called punishers. It is the latter changes, and particularly the timing of those changes, to which this chapter is devoted. Although the above definition of a punisher is relatively straightforward, in general punishers are misunderstood and the use of punishment is controversial in some circles.

Punishment is sometimes a natural consequence of behavior. Certain behaviors produce an aversive or unpleasant change in the environment, and as a result we are less likely to engage in those behaviors in the future. Although we might wish punishment were not a reality, without this type of consequence our lives would be considerably harder. On a hot summer day, asphalt can become dangerously hot. If a young boy was to walk outside without shoes, the child would experience a very aversive sensation on the soles of his feet. The painful punishing sensation has two effects. First, the boy immediately moves to the grass, which both terminates the painful sensation and prevents a more severe burn. Second, in the future the boy is less likely to go outside barefoot in the summer. Thus, although no one desires the boy to experience pain on his feet, experiencing this sensation helps prevent future bodily injury.

Our experiences with punishment may account for why we wear long pants and not shorts when walking through heavy brush, why we wear caps on a sunny day, why we stop at red lights instead of driving through them, and why we don't tell inappropriate jokes in front of certain audiences. Young children (upon skinning a knee for example) may exclaim how wonderful a life without physical pain might be. In fact, there are rare individuals who live just such a life, having a diagnosis of Congenital Insensitivity to Pain.

These individuals are unable to perceive physical pain. It should be unsurprising that this condition is far from the ideal a child might assume—these individuals generally have a greatly reduced life expectancy resulting from repeated injury (Sternbach, 1963). Without the aversive stimulation produced by engaging in certain behaviors, the behaviors that resulted in injury are not punished and thus persist, to the detriment of the child.

Punishment, of course, is by no means limited to physical pain. If I was to visit my grandmother and place my feet on the coffee table, I might promptly be scolded and told to remove my feet. Again, this scolding has two effects—I remove my feet and don't put my feet on the table in the future. Thus, although the sensations are quite different between the two examples (pain versus a scolding) both are effectively punishers as they decrease the future occurrences of the behaviors that produced those specific consequences.

IDIOSYNCRATIC AND TRANSITIVE EFFECTS

There are many misconceptions about punishment, and in common parlance punishment is often erroneously considered to be a way of "getting even" or seeking retribution against someone who engaged in an undesirable behavior. Moreover, the terms punisher and punishment conjure up mental images of specific items or actions; a spanking or being sent to one's room, for example, might float to mind if someone says, "Jerry was punished for cursing at the dinner table." Although a spanking or being sent to one's room may actually decrease the future likelihood of cursing at the dinner table (i.e., may function as a punisher), a punisher is defined by what it does to behavior rather than what it looks like. If, for example, Jerry had a television and video game system in his room, he might actually curse more in the future in order to be sent to his room. In this case, being sent to his room would function as a reinforcer, not a punisher. Conversely, things that might not commonly be considered punishers may actually function as such. Although Jerry might care deeply for his mother, a hug from her in front of his friends would likely decrease the future likelihood that Jerry would talk to his mother in the presence of his friends. Later in the day at home (and away from the eyes of his peers), however, a hug from his mother might function to actually increase the behavior it follows. This last example illustrates another important point regarding punishers—they may function as punishers on some occasions and not on others. Thus, it is incorrect to talk about certain actions (e.g., a spanking or a hug) as being punishers or not being punishers.

The only objective means of determining whether some action or event is or is not a punisher is by seeing whether it does or does not decrease the future likelihood of the behaviors it follows. And even then, that action or event may not always function as a punisher.

INFLUENCING A PUNISHERS EFFECTIVENESS

Although punishers are idiosyncratic and defined functionally (i.e., by their effect on behavior), not all punishers decrease behavior equally, and there are specific factors that can influence whether a punisher produces a large or small change in behavior. The most salient factors that influence a punisher's efficacy are a) intensity, with a more intense punisher having a greater suppressive effect than a less intense punisher, b) escapability, with inescapable punishers being more effective than escapable ones, c) schedule density, with punishers that occur every time the behavior occurs being more effective than those that only occur occasionally, d) competition with reinforcement, where a punisher is more effective if the behavior that produces punishment doesn't also produce reinforcement, e) removal and reintroduction, wherein a punisher's suppressive effect can often be heightened if the punisher is discontinued and then reintroduced, and f) immediacy, with immediate punishers being more effective than delayed punishers (Azrin and Holz, 1966; Lerman and Vorndran, 2002). Although each of these factors can alter the suppressive effect of a punisher, the immediacy of a punisher is perhaps the most influential element, and the timing of a punisher can be a critical determinant of whether a punisher is effective at all.

THE DELAY-OF-PUNISHMENT GRADIENT

Research on punishment timing has generally shown a clear relation between the immediacy of a punisher and its suppressive effect—immediate punishers are maximally effective, but there is a sharp drop in suppressive effect as the delay between the behavior and the delivery of the punisher increases. This change in suppression due to time delay has been referred to as the delay-of-punishment gradient (Kamin, 1959). Figure 1 shows the delay-of-punishment gradient representing hypothetical data.

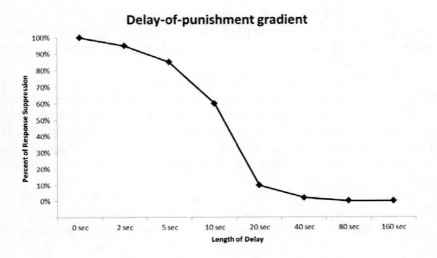

Figure 1. Delay-of-punishment gradient representing hypothetical data.

In this figure, a punisher that is delivered immediately (i.e., at 0 sec) is effective at suppressing 100% of future responding. As the delay gradually increases, however, the suppressive effect decreases. Moreover, this decrease in suppressive effect heightens as the delay lengthens such that eventually the punisher, although still delivered contingent on behavior, is wholly ineffective at suppressing behavior. This general pattern has been seen across a variety of species ranging from rats (Cairns and Perkins, 1972) and goldfish (Myer and Ricci, 1968) to humans (Trenholme and Baron, 1975). Although it appears that humans are generally better at mediating longer delays than other non-human animals, the gradient is still seen—as the delay increases, the suppressive effect decreases.

CONTINGENCY VERSUS CONTIGUITY

This decrease in a punisher's suppressive effect poses a significant problem for anyone attempting to change behavior with an intervention that includes a punishment component. Many teachers, parents, and clinicians program for a contingency between a behavior and some punishing consequence. If a student yells at a teacher, that student may receive detention. If a child hits a sibling, that child may be placed in time out.

If a client aggresses towards a staff member, the client may lose certain privileges. All of these consequences are intended to function as punishers, and in each case a contingency has been created between the problem behavior and the consequence.

The problem, however, is that although there may be a contingency between the behavior and consequence (i.e., there is a strong probability that the consequence will occur if the behavior occurs), there may be little temporal contiguity (i.e., the consequence may not occur immediately after the behavior). Although a contingency is necessary in a behavior change program, research on the delay-to-punish gradient shows that contiguity is also a critical factor.

One tempting solution is to simply suggest that these teachers, parents, or clinicians use only those punishers that can be immediately delivered. However, there are many practical reasons that punishers are delayed, particularly in non-laboratory settings. First, some punishers cannot be practically delivered in all settings. For example, a parent who uses time out as a consequence for hitting may find it difficult or impossible to deliver the consequence if the hitting occurs on a playground. Second, some behaviors are difficult to identify until long after they have occurred. Cheating, for example, is difficult to detect and, unless the cheater is caught in the act, punishment is nearly always delayed. Third, it may be unsafe for some staff to deliver a punishing consequence alone, thereby occasionally forcing a delay. Staff members who work with particularly aggressive clients, for example, may be unable to deliver a consequence until other staff members are present. Depending on the length of time until other staff arrive, this creates a delay between behavior and consequence delivery. Fourth, problem behavior may occur in the presence of individuals who are untrained or unauthorized to deliver the punishing consequence. For example, a babysitter might not be allowed to deliver the same punishers as a child's parent. The best a babysitter could do is report problem behavior to parents when they return, with punishment being delivered at that time. Each of these situations represents legitimate conditions under which immediate punishment is unlikely. The delay-of-punishment gradient, however, would indicate that such delayed punishers are less effective at best, and may be entirely ineffective.

Another concern with the use of delayed punishers is that although a delayed punisher is temporally distant from the behavior upon which it is contingent, it is temporally contiguous with some other behavior. It is possible, therefore, for a delayed punisher to decrease the behavior occurring immediately prior to the punisher's delivery.

Consider an example of a child stealing candy from a store and the stolen candy being discovered sometime later by his parents. The child is asked whether he stole the candy and replies truthfully that he did. The child then receives a scolding for stealing. In this scenario the response (i.e., stealing) occurred at some point in time but the punishing consequence (i.e., a scolding) was delivered much later.

In light of the delay-of-punishment gradient, the time delay between the theft and the scolding should render the scolding less effective (or ineffective) at decreasing future occurrences of stealing.

Furthermore, compared to responding decreased through immediate punishment, responding suppressed through delayed punishment is faster to recover (Azrin, 1956). Thus, a delayed punisher is less effective than an immediate punisher, and the levels of response suppression achieved are not as long lasting.

More problematic, however, is that the scolding occurred immediately after the child told the truth about stealing. Although there is no contingency between truth telling and the scolding, there is temporal contiguity which might decrease the future likelihood of telling the truth under similar circumstances. Although well-intentioned, the parents in this example may end up decreasing a behavior they want (being truthful) while doing nothing to affect the behavior they don't want (stealing).

The problem of delayed punishment is not a new concern. As early as 1930 the psychologist John B. Watson wrote "the idea that a child's future bad behavior will be prevented by giving him a licking in the evening for something he did in the morning is ridiculous. Equally ridiculous . . . is our legal and judicial method of punishment which allows a crime to be committed in one year and a punishment administered a year to two later" (p. 183). Despite the problems with delayed punishment, however, a parent, professional, or legal system is unlikely to allow problem behavior to go without a punishing consequence simply because there is a delay between the two events.

Yet, it is impractical to expect that all problem behavior can or will be immediately punished. The goal of the study of delayed punishers, then, should be to develop technologies to mediate the delay and improve the effectiveness of delayed punishers. To date little research has been directed towards this goal (Lerman and Vorndran, 2002; Meindl and Casey, 2012).

Although punishment is a natural consequence to some behaviors, there are (and rightly so) some ethical concerns regarding the use of punishment by one individual to change the behavior of another individual.

Particularly in regards to individuals with developmental disabilities and mental illnesses, history is replete with examples of punishers being used to decrease behaviors that could more ethically be changed through less aversive means such as reinforcement.

Nevertheless, punishers (of varying degrees of aversiveness) continue to be employed in a variety of settings (homes, schools, clinics, etc.) on a regular basis. From an ethical standpoint, if a punisher is to be used (detention, for example) it is crucial that the punisher effectively decrease the behavior upon which it was contingent. To deliver punishers that don't decrease these behaviors is to simply deliver aversive consequences with no hope of changing behavior. This is the concern with delayed punishers.

STRATEGIES FOR ALTERING THE DELAY-OF-PUNISHMENT GRADIENT

One important point to consider about the delay-of-punishment gradient is that, as seen in Figure 1, although there is a clear decrease in suppressive effect as the delay lengthens, it is only at the longer delays that the punisher becomes entirely ineffective. At shorter delays (10 s, for example) a punisher is rendered less effective, but it still exerts some suppressive effect. This raises the possibility that strategies could be developed that enhance a delayed punisher's suppressive effect.

The remainder of this chapter is devoted to presenting potential strategies for altering the delay-of-punishment gradient to improve the ability for a delayed punisher to suppress the behavior upon which it is contingent. Both basic and applied research related to each strategy will be discussed, but more research is needed on each strategy before they should be considered as well-established.

There are five specific strategies that have been studied in basic and applied research that might improve the efficacy of delayed punishment (Meindl and Casey, 2012). These are (a) to provide an immediate conditioned stimulus to bridge the delay to punishment, (b) to increase the intensity of the punisher, (c) to record and play back audio recordings of the response prior to the delivery of the punisher, (d) to have the individual reenact the response prior to delivery of the punisher, and (e) to provide explicit verbal instructions explaining the relation between the response and the punisher. In the following section, each of these strategies will be examined in detail.

Providing an Immediate Conditioned Stimulus

In situations where the delivery of immediate punishers is not possible or practical, one solution is to immediately deliver another consequence that signals that punishment will occur at a later time. A student who engages in problem behavior on the school bus en route to school might not be able to receive a timeout immediately. However, it would be possible to give the student a card or other signal (often referred to as a bridging stimulus) indicating that a timeout would occur once the child arrived at school. There is some evidence that such a procedure might enhance the effects of delayed punishment.

In a basic study on this topic, Tedford (1969) investigated the effects of bridging stimuli (cues) on the lever-pressing behavior of rats. In this study, 75 rats were divided into three different training groups, and exposed to different types of stimulus cues following lever presses. The study used operant chambers in which there were two response levers, dippers to deliver small amounts of a sucrose solution, and a chamber floor that was wired to provide a brief electric shock. For Group ND (nondifferentiated cues), responses on either of the two levers resulted in a brief blackout of the operant chamber lights. Thus, rats in this group experienced identical conditions after pressing the left or right lever. For Group L (light cues), responses on one lever produced pulsating lights, while responses on the other lever produced a brief blackout. For Group LT (light and tone cues), responses on one lever produced pulsating tones and pulsating light, while responses on the other lever produced a brief blackout. Thus, for Groups L and LT, the rats produced a distinctive lighting cue depending which lever they pressed. Initially, responding on either lever produced reinforcement (sucrose solution) for all groups. Once the rats had learned to press each lever, they were divided into 5 subgroups. For four of the subgroups, pressing the previously preferred lever resulted in punishment (brief electric shock), delivered after a specific delay (1.25, 5, 20, or 80 s). A fifth subgroup of rats served as a control group and did not receive any punishment. Groups L and LT, who were exposed to a distinctive cue immediately following each lever-press, displayed more suppression of responding than Group ND, across all delay lengths. This was particularly evident at the longest delay (80 s), at which Group ND showed no decrease in responding on the targeted lever, whereas responding by Groups L and LT did show a decrease. These results suggest that cues delivered immediately following a response can increase the effectiveness of a delayed punisher.

This finding has been supported by applied research as well, most notably in a study by Altman and Krupshaw (1983). In this study, the authors evaluated a delayed overcorrection procedure designed to decrease the frequency of mild and severe tantrums by a 14-year-old boy. A delayed punishment procedure was deemed necessary due to the fact that the boy's father was the only person in his family who could successfully enforce an effective punishment procedure, but was often unavailable due to his work schedule. To bridge this delay, an X was written on a calendar immediately following an instance of tantrum behavior, and a 40-60 min overcorrection procedure was then implemented upon the father's return from work. Actual lengths of the delay to punishment in this study varied, ranging from 10 min to 96 hr, with a median delay of 5.5 hr. Using a multiple baseline design where the intervention was introduced in a staggered fashion, the researchers implemented the delayed punishment procedure first on severe tantrum behavior, after which there was an immediate suppression of the behavior (from 1.0 per week to 0.1 per week). Mild tantrums continued to occur with some frequency until the procedure was implemented on that behavior, after which a similar reduction was observed. Suppression of both mild and severe tantrum responses were maintained during a 1-year follow-up.

There are at least two possible conceptual explanations for the suppressive effect of presenting stimuli immediately following behavior to signal upcoming but delayed punishment. First, it is possible that such cues act as conditioned punishers. Stimuli that reliably precede the delivery of a punisher can become punishers themselves through repeated pairing. Thus, in the study by Altman and Krupshaw (1983), one might hypothesize that having someone write an X on the calendar became an effective consequence in its own right due to its frequently preceding the punishment procedure (recall that occasionally the delayed punisher occurred only 10 min after writing the X). A second explanation for the effects of such stimuli is that cues permit an organism to discriminate the time delay between the response and the punisher. In this regard, cues might be considered compound stimuli, involving both the stimulus itself and the passage of time. A study by Bitterman (1964) illustrates how such a stimulus might operate. Goldfish were exposed to a classical conditioning procedure in which a conditioned stimulus (CS) of a light was presented followed by an unconditioned stimulus (US) of shock, after a specified delay that ranged from 1 s to 27 s. After conditioning, goldfish that experienced a short delay (i.e., 1 s) between light and shock engaged in a conditioned response (CR) of increased movement immediately upon the presentation of the CS.

However, goldfish that experienced a long delay (i.e., 27 s) between the light and the shock engaged in the CR only after a period of time elapsed following the presentation of the CS. A similar effect should presumably occur with delayed punishment involving a bridging cue, in that an aversive stimulus (the punisher) reliably occurs following at some interval after the cue. The presence of such a compound stimulus could improve the suppressive effects of delayed punishers by improving discrimination of the time delay. This would account for the finding reported by Tedford (1969), in that the cue presented to rats in Groups L and LT improved discrimination of the time delay they experienced between pressing the lever and receiving a shock.

Increasing the Intensity of the Delayed Punisher

Basic research on punishment has demonstrated that when delivered immediately after a response, more intense punishers have a stronger suppressive effect on responding than less intense punishers (Azrin and Holz, 1966). There is evidence that this may also be true for delayed punishers. If so, one way practitioners might increase the effects of delayed punishers would be to simply use punishers of a higher intensity. For example, if a response cost procedure was being used, and one token was taken away immediately each time the student engaged in a target behavior, that might be sufficient. However, to achieve a similar result with a delayed punishment procedure, the cost associated with the response might need to be greater (e.g., taking away several tokens).

Myer and Ricci (1968) studied the phenomenon with goldfish that were initially trained to engage in a feeding response. In a subsequent phase, they were exposed to contingent shock at one of five delay lengths (0, 2.5, 5, 10, and 20 s). The voltage of the shocks was increased incrementally until the feeding response was suppressed completely. As the delay to punishment increased, the intensity of shock required to suppress responding also increased. When shock intensity was high enough, complete suppression was achieved, even at the longest delays. This was confirmed by a second experiment, in which goldfish were exposed to either low intensity (10 v) or high intensity (25 v) shock, at one of three delay lengths (0, 5, or 10 s). Whereas the low intensity shock produced a traditional delay-of-punishment gradient, the high intensity shock produced similar levels of suppression across all delay lengths.

It is important to note that increasing punisher intensity has not been studied in applied research on delayed punishment. This may be in part due to the types of manipulations required to demonstrate such an effect. The types of punishers used in applied settings are not always easy to quantify according to intensity, and delivering punishment in a sufficiently controlled manner to perform controlled research of this kind may not be practical or ethical. However, the basic research does seem to highlight a variable that has significant impact on the efficacy of delayed punishment, which bears consideration by teachers, parents, and others who might use such procedures.

An explanation for the increased suppressive effect of more intense punishers is that when a high-intensity punisher is used, there may be a general suppressive effect on many behaviors, not simply the behavior that immediately preceded the punisher (Mazur, 2002). This could account for the fact that a delayed high-intensity punisher suppresses a target response that did not occur in close temporal proximity to the delivery of the consequence. For example, if a child receives a sharp verbal reprimand following an instance of hitting a sibling, the effect might be not only to decrease the likelihood of hitting, but of other responses that occurred prior to that target behavior (e.g., approaching and playing with the sibling). The general suppression effect is not necessarily a problem, so long as the responses being suppressed are ones that we want to decrease. However, it does highlight the possibility that such an approach could have unintended side effects.

Replaying Recordings of the Target Behavior

Another method of increasing the suppressive effects of delayed punishment is to record the occurrence of the target behavior, and then replay the event for the individual at a later time, immediately before delivering the punisher. Thus, if a child were to scream during a community outing, and the teacher was unable to implement a timeout procedure at that time, it might be possible to record the child's scream on audio or video, and then replay it later when it is possible to deliver the consequence. Doing so would have the advantage of ensuring that key stimuli associated with the target response were present immediately prior to the delivery of the punisher.

Although basic researchers have not studied this method, some applied studies have supported the potential utility of playing back audio recordings during the delivery of delayed punishment (Goncalves, Iwata, and Chiang, 1983; Rolider and Van Houten, 1985).

Rolider and Van Houten (1985) employed a multiple baseline design to study this treatment approach with a 5-year-old boy who engaged in tantrum behaviors across different locations. The experimenters tape-recorded the boy's tantrums and then later played back 1 min segments of the recording during which the target behavior had occurred. They then immediately implemented a 20 s movement-suppression procedure. The procedure had a significant suppressive effect, with tantrums reducing to near-zero levels. When the treatment was discontinued briefly, tantrums increased, and then were once again brought down to acceptable levels when the intervention was re-introduced. In a second experiment, Rolider and Van Houten compared the effects of such a procedure to an alternative condition in which the audio was played back, but no punisher was delivered. For both of the boys in this study, acceptable levels of suppression of tantrum behavior were achieved only when the audio playback included delayed punishment.

One way of explaining the effects of such a recording procedure would be that the equipment used to record the target behavior might come to serve as a discriminative stimulus or cue indicating punishment contingencies are in place. This notion is supported by the data reported by Rolider and Van Houten, in that when the procedure was implemented across environments, the suppressive effect was more immediate in the second and third settings than it was in the first setting. Such a pattern would be consistent with a discriminative stimulus interpretation, in that the tape recorder may have acquired such a discriminative function when used in the first setting, and thus had an immediate suppressive effect when introduced in subsequent locations. In essence, the sight of the tape recorder may have been sufficient to signal to the student that a delayed punishment contingency was in place whereby tantrum behavior would result in an aversive movement-suppression procedure.

Another explanation for the suppressive effect of replaying recordings might be that by presenting the recording in close temporal proximity to the movement suppression procedure, the sounds on the recording became conditioned punishers.

Essentially, these sounds were paired with punishment. If the stimuli produced by engaging in the problem behavior (e.g., the sounds of a tantrum) were to become conditioned punishers, this could serve to suppress responses that produce those stimuli (e.g., tantrums). For example, a child who curses inappropriately might be recorded on audio engaging in the target behavior, and then have the audio played back immediately before the delivery of a punisher (e.g., a reprimand).

The child would hear the curse word, and then immediately experience an aversive consequence, potentially causing "hearing a curse word" to become a conditioned aversive stimulus. If the student were to later curse, this would produce that same aversive stimulus, and thus have a suppressive effect on the behavior.

Reenacting the Problem Behavior at the Time of Punishment

Another method for circumventing the possible disadvantages of delayed punishment is to have the individual reenact their inappropriate behavior immediately before experiencing the delayed punisher. In this way, punishment can be administered in close temporal proximity to an instance of the target behavior, albeit one that has been evoked in an artificial manner. For example, if a child were to engage in aggression on the playground, a teacher might not be able to immediately deliver an appropriate consequence. Instead, the teacher might have the student act out the aggressive behavior again once they have returned to the classroom, at which time an immediate punisher could be presented.

In this way, it might be possible to ensure that there is closer temporal contiguity between response and punisher, and a stronger link might be made between the consequence and the response it is intended to decrease.

In an applied study, Van Houten and Rolider (1988) used such a procedure to target the problem behavior of two individuals: a 4-year old boy with autism, and a 17-year old girl with a developmental delay.

Following a period of observation, a delayed punishment procedure was implemented in which the target behavior (foot stomping, biting, or stealing) was reenacted.

For example, if the child had engaged in foot stomping during the previous observation, the experimenter would bring in the individual whose foot had been stepped upon, and guide the aggressing child's foot over it to recreate the initial event prior to delivering a movement-suppression timeout procedure. The delayed punishment plus reenactment intervention was effective in suppressing all target behaviors to near-zero levels, and this effect was maintained at a 4-month follow-up observation.

The most obvious explanation for the effects of reenacting the target behavior during delayed punishment is that the punisher is being delivered in close temporal contiguity to an instance of the challenging behavior (i.e., the reenactment).

In this regard, one could conceptualize this as a schedule involving intermittent punishment, in that some but not all instances of the behavior produce the consequence. For participants in the study by Van Houten and Rolider, instances of the target behaviors that occurred during the observation period did not produce any immediate consequence, but instances that occurred during the reenactment sessions that followed resulted in punishment. Although such schedules are not as effective as continuous schedules at suppressing responding, they can result in some degree of suppression, and could account for the suppressive effects of reenactments during delayed punishment.

Providing Explicit Verbal Instructions

Another way that one can bridge the delay to punishment is to include verbal instructions regarding the contingency between the behavior and the delayed punisher. For example, if an adult with developmental disabilities engages in problem behavior (e.g., property destruction) during a community outing, this individual might experience a delayed punisher (e.g., loss of tokens) upon their return home, along with a verbal instruction stating why the tokens were being taken away. In this way, practitioners can potentially clear up some of the ambiguity inherent in a delayed punishment, by laying out the contingencies in a verbal rule.

In a basic study, Verna (1977) examined the use of verbal instructions during delayed punishment with a group of 4th grade students. Students were divided into three groups: immediate punishment, delayed punishment with minimal instructions, and delayed punishment with specific instructions. During experimental sessions, students were left alone to play with a toy gun that had been rigged to break at a specific time. Upon the breaking of the toy, students in the immediate punishment group were immediately told that because they had broken the toy they were to forfeit a token they had earned previously. For the delayed punishment conditions, students were taken out of the room, and then brought back 4 hours later, at which time verbal instructions were given and the token was taken away. In the minimal instruction group, students received only a vague explanation of why the token was lost (e.g., "Because of what happened earlier, I have to take your token away."). In the specific instruction group, students were told that the token was being taken away because they had broken the toy gun earlier. After this, all students were left alone with a similar toy gun.

To evaluate suppression of the play response, the experimenters measured the latency with which the students approached the toy gun, the duration for which they engaged with it, and how many times they used the toy gun. Levels of suppression were high and roughly equal for the immediate punishment and the delayed punishment plus specific instruction groups, whereas the delayed punishment plus minimal instruction group played more with the toy gun, indicating less effective punishment.

In a related applied study, Jackson, Salzberg, Pacholl, and Dorsey (1981) described a procedure to reduce the aggressive and disruptive behavior of a 10-year-old boy with a behavior disorder. These aggressive and disruptive behaviors occurred so often during the student's bus ride to and from school that he was at risk for being excluded from that service. A procedure was implemented during which the bus driver collected data on the frequency of problem behavior during that day's commute, and reported this information to the student's parents, who then delivered a punisher involving the loss of privileges (e.g., watching television) if the total number of problem behaviors exceeded a specified value. Verbal instructions were presented at the beginning of the intervention, outlining the contingencies that were in place, and the criteria for loss of privileges. This intervention resulted in a significant reduction of the target behavior, suggesting that the delayed punisher combined with verbal instructions was effective in suppressing the student's disruptive and aggressive behavior on the bus.

One explanation for the effects of verbal instructions is that the verbal rule may enhance the individual's ability to discriminate relevant environmental stimuli related to the contingency between the behavior and the delayed punisher. A verbal instruction might alter the function of the stimuli specified (i.e., those associated with engaging in the target response), by associating them with a punishing consequence.

For the students in the study by Verna (1977), the toy gun may have become a discriminative stimulus or cue indicating the likelihood of punishment due to the inclusion of a specific verbal instruction. The toy gun could then come to have a suppressive effect on responding, even though punishment was never delivered in its actual presence. If, for example, upon petting a neighborhood dog a young child was told that the dog was particularly vicious and would bite the child if petted, the dog may come to function as a punisher. The future likelihood that the child would pet the dog would likely decrease. The dog never bit the child, but the dog changed from a reinforcer to a punisher, and also became a cue for possible punishment (i.e., biting).

Another way of understanding the effects of verbal instructions would be that additional verbal responses (possibly covert) might occur as the result of hearing the rule. For example, a parent might tell a child that if she refuses to eat her vegetables, she will lose the opportunity to have dessert. If the child later begins to refuse to eat the vegetables, she might emit verbal responses such as "if I eat my whole dinner, I will get my dessert." Such stimuli could then serve as immediate consequences or prompts to discourage the refusal of vegetables.

WHAT DON'T WE KNOW?

The five strategies described in this chapter are intended only to serve as loose guides for practitioners and researchers. Although there is some evidence supporting each strategy, only a handful of studies have been conducted regarding each strategy, and no strategy is well-established in the literature as effective at increasing the suppressive effect of a delayed punisher. Further, there is much about each strategy that remains unknown, and there are problems with the supporting research.

Chief among the unknown effects of each strategy is whether the delayed punisher affects the behaviors it immediately follows rather than only those upon which it is contingent.

In a delayed punishment scenario, a person emits some behavior and a punisher occurs after some delay. A child, for example, curses during dinner and is not allowed dessert afterwards. In the period of time between the cursing and being denied dessert, the child does not cease to behave, of course, but rather engages in a range of behaviors (some appropriate, some inappropriate). The child talks about his day, asks questions of his parents, expresses dislike for a certain food item, sings a short song, etc. In developing a strategy to minimize the delay-of-punishment gradient, there are two primary outcomes that should be generated. First, the strategy should enable a delayed punisher to affect the future probability of the behavior upon which it is contingent.

In this instance, the strategy should enable the denial of dessert to decrease the likelihood of cursing at the table in the future. Second, the strategy should enable the delayed punisher to effectively "ignore" the behaviors upon which it is not contingent. In this instance, the denial of dessert should not affect the future likelihood of talking, questioning, singing, or any other behavior that did not produce the denial of dessert.

In the research supporting each of the five strategies discussed in this chapter, there is some evidence that the first outcome is produced, but there is no evidence that the second outcome is obtained. That is to say, as of yet there is no evidence that any strategy discussed in this chapter will "ignore" the behaviors that occur immediately before the delayed punisher is presented. If a delayed punisher decreases the behaviors with which it is temporally contiguous, but not contingent, this would call the use of delayed punishment into serious question as appropriate behaviors might be negatively affected in the process of decreasing inappropriate behaviors.

In addition to some unknown effects of delayed punishment, there are also some problems with the research on delayed punishment—most critically, there is very little. Although punishment is a natural process and vital to learning, and although punishment of some form is common in almost every setting, very little research has been devoted to examining the affects of punishment on behavior the last several decades. The bulk of the basic research on punishment was conducted in the 60's and 70's (Pierce and Cheney, 2013) at which point research began to slow considerably. A similar decline in publications on the topic has occurred in the realm of applied research. This dwindling of research on punishment was not a result of our learning everything there is to know about punishment (consider the number of unanswered questions in this chapter alone). Rather, this shift away from research on punishment is partly the result of university review boards (those responsible for approving or denying proposed research projects), who were in turn influenced by changing public opinion on punishment research. Conducting a study on punishment, either applied or basic, requires some organism to be exposed, often repeatedly, to some aversive event in order to observe changes in that organism's behavior. Although punishment research can produce meaningful and applicable information, public concerns about the welfare of human and animal participants, and outrage over cases in which punishers have been misused, has made it more difficult for researchers to study punishment. The result is that researchers and practitioners alike are often left relying on relatively older basic and applied research to inform their practices.

There are strengths and weaknesses with the existing basic and applied research on this topic. The available basic research on delayed punishment has an advantage over applied research in that the basic research is generally more methodologically rigorous. The delay lengths are typically tightly controlled, the punishers used are easily quantifiable (e.g., 5 v shock versus 25 v shock), and there are frequent component analyses.

These component analyses are particularly important as they allow for an examination the effects of a delayed punisher both with and without a specific strategy. The biggest problems with the available basic research relates to the generality of the findings. Most basic research has employed relatively intense punishers (i.e., high voltage shock) over relatively short delays (i.e., on the order of seconds to minutes), which are unlike those conditions in which punishment is likely to be used in most applied settings. Thus, although the available basic research is methodologically rigorous, it is questionable whether the effects found in a basic research study would be replicated with human subjects using less intense punishers and longer delays.

The applied research on delayed punishers has strengths and weaknesses that are almost the exact opposite of those found in the basic realm. The generality of the findings of applied research is usually less questionable as such research is frequently conducted with humans subject, in "real world" environments, and with commonplace punishers. However, the vast majority of the applied studies on delayed punishers are methodologically much weaker than the basic studies.

In most of the applied studies on the topic, time delays were uncontrolled (sometimes with very large ranges) and researchers rarely examined the separate and combined effects of a strategy and delayed punisher. Thus, although the applied research may have more applicability to different people in different places, the conclusions that can be drawn are less concrete than those drawn from basic research.

What is needed is first and foremost more research on the effects of punishment, particularly delayed punishment. The timing of punishment is a critical factor to achieving a suppressive effect, and punishers are routinely delayed in applied settings.

More specifically, however, what is needed is translational research on punishment that operates in the area between applied and basic research. Translational research takes the findings of basic research and attempts to examine their application in practical or "real world" settings. This type of research generally possesses the methodological strengths of basic research, but incorporates analogs of the natural settings or situations in which delayed punishment might occur. This type of approach would enable researchers to study delayed punishment in a controlled, meaningful, and ethically sound manner, and to more easily extrapolate those findings to clinical utility.

Although there is some research to suggest the potential effectiveness of each strategy discussed in this chapter, the boundaries and conditions under which they are effective are almost wholly unknown.

These strategies, however, could function as starting points for investigating methods to minimize the delay-of-punishment gradient and improve the clinical effectiveness of delayed punishers. It is hoped that identifying these strategies might spur more research on delayed punishment and punishment in general. A lack of research on punishment does not decrease the likelihood that punishment will be used, but it does decrease the likelihood that it will be used effectively and ethically. Whenever a person engages in a behavior, changes are produced in the environment. Some of these changes decrease the likelihood of that behavior in the future—to ignore this type of change is to ignore an important aspect of learning, and we do so at our own peril.

REFERENCES

Altman, K. and Krupshaw, R. (1983). Suppressing aggressive-destructive behavior by delayed overcorrection. *Journal of Behavior Therapy and Experimental Psychiatry,* 14, 359–362.

Azrin, N. H. (1956). Effects of two intermittent schedules of immediate and nonimmediate punishment. *Journal of Psychology,* 42, 3–21.

Azrin, N. H. and Holz, W. C. (1966). Punishment. In: W. K. Honig (Ed.), *Operant Behavior: Areas of research and application* (pp. 380–447). New York: Appleton-Century-Crofts.

Bitterman, M. E. (1964). Classical conditioning in the goldfish as a function of the CS-US interval. *Journal of Comparative and Physiological Psychology,* 58, 359–366.

Cairns, G. F. and Perkins, C. C. (1972). Delay of punishment and choice behavior in the rat. *Journal of Comparative and Physiological Psychology,* 79, 438–442.

Goncalves, S. J., Iwata, B. A. and Chiang, S. J. (1983). Assessment and training of supervisors' evaluative feedback to their staff in an operant learning program for handicapped children. *Education and Treatment of Children,* 6, 11–20.

Jackson, A. T., Salzberg, C. L., Pacholl, B., and Dorsey, D. S. (1981). The comprehensive rehabilitation of a behavior problem child in his home and community. *Education and Treatment of Children,* 4, 195–215.

Kamin, L. J. (1959). The delay-of-punishment gradient. *Journal of Comparative and Physiological Psychology,* 52, 434–437.

Lerman, D. C. and Vorndran, C. M. (2002). On the status of knowledge for using punishment: Implications for treating behavior disorders. *Journal of Applied Behavior Analysis,* 35, 4312–4464.

Mazur, J. E. (2002). *Learning and behavior* (5th ed.). Upper Saddle River, NJ: Prentice Hall.

Meindl, J. N. and Casey, L. G. (2012). Increasing the suppressive effect of delayed punishers: A review of basic and applied literature. *Behavioral Interventions,* 27, 129–150.

Myer, J. S. and Ricci, D. (1968). Delay of punishment gradients for the goldfish. *Journal of Comparative and Physiological Psychology,* 66, 417–421.

Rolider, A. and Van Houten, R. (1985). Suppressing tantrum behavior in public places through the use of delayed punishment mediated by audio recordings. *Behavior Therapy,* 16, 181–194.

Pierce, W. D. and Cheney, C. D. (2013). *Behavior Analysis and Learning* (5th ed.). New York, NY: Taylor and Francis

Sternbach, R. A. (1963). Congenital insensitivity to pain: A critique. *Psychological Bulletin,* 60, 252–264.

Tedford, W. H. (1969). Effect of delayed punishment upon choice behavior in the white rat. *Journal of Comparative and Physiological Psychology,* 69, 673–676.

Trenholme, I. A. and Baron, A. (1975). Immediate and delayed punishment of human behavior by loss of reinforcement. *Learning and Motivation,* 6, 62–79.

Van Houten, R. and Rolider, A. (1988). Recreating the scene: An effective way to provide delayed punishment for inappropriate motor behavior. *Journal of Applied Behavior Analysis,* 21, 187–192.

Verna, G. B. (1977). The effects of four-hour delay of punishment under two conditions of verbal instruction. *Child Development,* 48, 621–624.

Watson, J. B. (1930). *Behaviorism.* New York: W. W. Norton and Company, Inc.

In: Psychology of Punishment
Editor: Nicolas Castro

ISBN: 978-1-62948-103-6
© 2013 Nova Science Publishers, Inc.

Chapter 5

CORPORAL PHYSICAL PUNISHMENT TODAY: THE HISTORY, EFFECTS AND LONG-TERM IMPLICATIONS

J. D. Barton[1], Adam Kaplan[1], Natalia Moss[2] and Judy Ho[1]

[1]Pepperdine University, Los Angeles, CA
[2]University of New Mexico, Albuquerque, NM

ABSTRACT

Physical punishment, an ancient practice, has been the locus of recent discussion, research, and legislation. This chapter will explore corporal punishment in the United States, and review research that addresses the practices' effect on short and long term mental health. In addition to discussing discrepant prevalence rates and professional and public opinions, this chapter will address the connection between physical punishment and clinically diagnosable disorders, and other related mental health and well-being factors. Recommendations will be made regarding how to educate parents and encourage effective behavioral management, with a special emphasis on noting important risk and protective factors for the detrimental effects of corporal punishment on youth. Finally, the United States' hesitance to legislate against corporal punishment will be explored, and the negative effects of its proliferation will be discussed.

INTRODUCTION

"He who spares his rod hates his son, but he who loves him disciplines him promptly" (Proverbs 24:13 New King James Version). Corporal punishment has existed for centuries. This controversial practice continues to be an issue of concern for many including parents, teachers, and legislators. Modern psychological research and discourse allows scientists to explore the proximal and distal effects of corporal punishment. This chapter aims to describe the extant research on corporal punishment with youth and how it affects mental health and well-being, review professional and public opinions on the subject, and discuss risk and protective factors and recommendations for therapists working with families.

DEFINING PHYSICAL PUNISHMENT

Physical punishment involving children, also known as corporal punishment, is a parenting, teaching, and authoritarian practice that was once ubiquitous in the United States and abroad, and remains prevalent today (Gersoff, 2010). Although exact parameters for physical punishment differ according to culture and region, physical punishment is often defined as open hand hitting that is not intended to injure, but rather is designed to modify child behavior (Gersoff, 2010). The United Nation's Children's Fund (UNICEF) defines corporal punishment as " the use of physical force causing pain, not wounds, as a means of discipline" (UNICEF awareness campaign). UNICEF believes that corporal punishment lowers self-esteem, teaches children to be victims, and hinders the learning process (UNICEF).

Physical Punishment is becoming increasingly regarded as an act of violence against children (Zolotar, Theodore, Runyun, Chang & Laskey, 2010). Research suggests that physical punishment can impede intellectual development and predict certain externalizing behaviors such as anger and impulsivity as well as internalizing behaviors like withdrawal (Berlin et al., 2009). While corporal punishment is on the decline globally, the practice remains prevalent in the United States (Hess, Gray & Nunez, 2012). The number of countries that legislate against corporal punishment at home as a behavioral management technique is increasing (Zoltar et al., 2010) in accordance with the recommendations of the United Nations Convention on the Rights of the Child (Zoltar et al. 2010). The convention advocated for states to take 'all appropriate legislative, administrative, social, and educational measures to protect the child from all forms of physical or mental violence' (UNICEF, 1989; Article 19). Corporal punishment, by its various definitions, can be conceptualized by a form of physical as well as a form of mental violence based on its documented effects. Yet, the U.S. and Somalia are the only two countries that have yet to abide by the United Nations' recommendations on this matter.

Physical Punishment in the US

Estimates of the prevalence of physical punishment in the United States vary greatly, in part because of a lack of standardized definition. When Afifi et al. (2012) used data from the National Epidemiological Survey on Alcohol and Related Conditions to investigate a representative population of 34,653 Americans, the research found the rate of physical punishment to be approximately 6%. This is markedly lower than other samples of the general population, which estimate the prevalence of physical punishment to be between 48% and 80% (Afifi, Brownridge, Cox, & Sareen, 2006; MacMillan et al., 1999). Afifi and colleagues (2012) believe this is because they had stricter criteria for physical punishment and only included "physical punishment cases in the absence of more several types of more severe child maltreatment" such as sexual abuse, emotional abuse, and physical neglect. Gersoff (2010) estimates that 50% of American toddlers, and 65 to 68% of American preschoolers are subjected to corporal punishment as a regular method of parental discipline. Gersoff states that "by the time American children reach middle and high school, eighty-five percent have been physically punished by their parents" (Gersoff, 2010). Similarly, a study of 649 American college students approximates that 40% of participants had experienced some sort of corporal punishment by the time they were 13 years old (Turner, 2004).

PROFESSIONAL VS. PUBLIC OPINIONS

Regardless of the exact statistics, many American psychologists believe that eliminating corporal punishment is a moral imperative. Lenta (2012) states physical punishment is "morally wrong" and "ought to be illegal" (p.690). According to Gersoff (2010), "… the risks for substantial harm from corporal punishment outweigh any benefit of immediate child compliance" (p. 32). The American Academy of Pediatrics advises against striking or spanking a child of any age (Shelov, Altman, 2009). Some Americans, however, continue to view corporal punishment, especially spanking, as a valid parenting practice. When Hess et al. (2012) queried 206 undergraduate students enrolled at an American university, they found that 75% of participants viewed hitting a child as a valid method of punishment rather than a form of physical abuse.

Physical Punishment and Psychological Well-Being

Corporal punishment administered in several stages of development has been repeatedly linked to a number of negative outcomes. A cohort study of children from 20 large U.S. cities found frequent use of corporal punishment (defined in the study as spanking a child twice or more per month) found increased aggressive behavior in children who have endured corporal punishment (Taylor, Mangarella, Lee & Rice, 2010). Callendar, Olson, Choe & Sameroff (2011) assessed 245 young children and found this type of punishment on three-year-olds was associated with increased levels of aggression when children were reassessed at five years of age. Similarly, frequent physical punishment during preschool years has been found to predict higher levels of externalized problem behaviors in kindergarten (Calendar et al., 2012). Landsford et al. (2010) found that there were bi-directional associations between higher levels of externalizing behaviors in boys and girls ages 6-9 and more frequent parental physical. Specifically, higher externalizing behaviors in one year led to more frequent physical punishment in the subsequent year, and more frequent physical punishment also lead to higher externalizing behaviors in the subsequent year. These results are suggestive of a negative, exacerbating cycle between youth problem behaviors and parental use of physical discipline. While genetics may predispose children to externalized behaviors, Boutwell et al. (2011) observed "children exposed to increased use of corporal punishment exhibited increased behavioral problems, even after controlling for the influence of genetic factors" (p.565). These results provide further evidence that the use of corporal punishment may play an important role in the youths' development of problematic behaviors.

Fatori et al.'s (2013) cross sectional surveys showed physical punishment to be linked to childhood and adolescent behavioral and mental health problems as assessed by several self-report and parent-report questionnaires. Not only has physical punishment shown to predict mood disorders, anxiety disorders, and drug and alcohol abuse (Afifi, 2012) but it has also been found to prime parents to commit acts of physical abuse (Gersoff, 2010), perhaps because the youth are emotionally and behaviorally difficult to manage. Importantly, Appleton and Stanley (2011) warn parents to be aware of the "dangers of physical punishment escalating into physical abuse".

Physical Punishment, in the absence of physical abuse, emotional abuse, physical neglect, or emotional neglect, still places youth at elevated risk for developing Axis 1 and Axis 2 disorders according to the criteria of the DSM-IV-TR (Afifi, 2012).

These researchers documented elevated rates of depression, dysthymia, mania, and hypomania in those who experienced physical punishment as children (Afifi, 2012). Turner and Muller (2004) also found that corporal punishment, independent of other history of abuse, is positively correlated with depressive symptoms. Afifi et al. (2012) found when analyzing their data after it was adjusted for sociodemographic variables that "harsh physical punishment was associated with an increased likelihood of several personality disorders" (p.187). The researchers reported a 4% to 7% reduction in personality disorders if physical punishment in the absence of child maltreatment did not occur (Afifi, 2012).

International research offers additional supporting evidence that physical punishment is detrimental to a child's psychological wellbeing. The majority of studies that surveyed children in developing countries found a relationship between physical punishment and youth physical and emotional pain (Sanapo et al., 2011). Researchers in China have discovered an association between physical punishment in early childhood and alcoholism later in life (Cheng et al, 2010).

A study of 919 adolescents in Santiago, Chile found that both frequent and infrequent parental use of corporal punishment predicts delinquent and aggressive behavior in adolescents. (Ma et al., 2010). A cross-sectional study conducted in the city of Embo in southeast Brazil which utilized a high-risk, low socioeconomic sample found that severe physical punishment was related to child mental health internalizing problems including withdrawal and externalizing problems including such as aggression in disadvantaged communities (Bordin et al., 2009). A study of deaf children in Norway indicated corporal punishment was a significant risk factor for mental health problems such as depression, anxiety or fearfulness later in life (Kvam & Loeb, 2009). Kim Oates, an Australian researcher, believes that physical punishment not only puts children at risk for exhibiting aggressive and antisocial behavior, but it also tacitly endorses future illegal acts of violence (Oates, 2011).

In addition to contributing to diagnosable mental health disorders, it is clear from extant literature that physical punishment is associated with maladaptive responses that negatively reverberate throughout the lifespan.

Recommendations

As discussed above, corporal punishment has been found to negatively impact the psychological well-being of children both immediately and long-term. It is important take steps to educate parents on the lasting effects of physical punishment and provide them with more effective alternatives to behaviorally manage children.

There are several interventions that have demonstrated effectiveness for a variety of youth emotional and behavioral problems that have shown benefits when applied to youth who have been exposed to physical punishment. Parent-child interaction therapy (PCIT) is an empirically supported treatment to enhance the parent-child relationship and to help parents learn how to effectively manage disruptive behavior in young children. It draws on components of developmental, attachment, and social learning theories and integrates operant conditioning concepts with the relational focus of play therapy (Eyberg, 2004). When applied to families that use physical punishment, the frequency of corporal punishment was reduced and the incidence of more effective parenting strategies rose (Eyberg, 2005; Urquiza & McNeil, 1996; Pearl, 2008). Parent training programs are based on the premise that parents will be less likely to physically and/or emotionally abuse a child if they improve their child-rearing skills, expand their repertoire of responses to children's problematic behaviors, modify attitudes linked to harsh parenting, and rely less on coercive behavior management strategies (Lundahl, Nimer, & Parsons, 2006). Many parent training programs also include components to address parents' emotional well-being and teach effective coping skills for anger and stress (Lundahl, Nimer, & Parsons, 2006). In a meta-analysis of 23 parent training programs that were designed to reduce or prevent physical punishment and child abuse or neglect, these programs resulted in improvements in parental attitudes and emotional adjustment and child rearing skills, and decreased incidences of documented abuse (Lundahl, Nimer, & Parsons, 2006).

In addition, the inclusion of a behavioral component and conducting parent training sessions both at the therapist's office and in the home significantly enhanced the effectiveness (Lundahl, Nimer, & Parsons, 2006). Early intervention is key, as research suggests that working with the family when the youth is young (e.g., between ages 0-8 years) can decrease risk behaviors before problematic behaviors become crystallized (Webster-Stratton & Taylor, 2001).

A widely disseminated and tested public health campaign, the Triple P-Positive Parenting Program, strengthens parenting through five levels of intervention that varies in delivery, modality and intensity of service to more specifically address the problems of each individual family (Nowak & Heinrichs, 2008). Triple P is based on social learning theory and utilizes five principles to teach positive parenting: (a) ensuring a safe and engaging environment, (b) creating a positive learning environment, (c) using assertive discipline, (d) having realistic expectations, and (e) taking care of oneself as a parent. Triple P empowers the parent to believe that he can improve the behavior of his child through his own actions, and helps him to become confident in decision-making and problem solving (Barth, 2009). Barth (2009) states that this campaign has demonstrated substantial promise in several large national and international trials for encouraging effective parenting. This multifaceted parenting campaign has demonstrated substantial promise in several large trials.

In addition to educating parents and providing them with more effective child management strategies, therapists should be aware of some of the factors believed to mediate the effects of physical punishment so that they can also be specifically addressed as part of therapy. Turner and Muller (2004) believe that frequency and form of punishment, race, parental monitoring, normative levels of corporal punishment, and parental anger can "buffer or accentuate the impact of corporal punishment." Culture should be taken into account as some minorities and lower income families are "more approving of the use of corporal punishment, tend to use more corporal punishment, and are less prone to the deleterious effects of corporal punishment" (Turner & Muller, p. 764).

Turner and Muller (2004) "suggest that parental anger during corporal punishment likely reflects impulsiveness and loss of control; that is, it is reasonable to assume that parents who are very angry when administering discipline are more likely to spank impulsively, exhibit less control, and are less likely to incorporate reasoning than when they administer corporal punishment without anger" (p. 765). In addition, special caution should be taken when the mother appears to issue the punishment impulsively as this may result in antisocial behavior in the child.

RISK AND PROTECTIVE FACTORS

As this chapter has illustrated, childhood exposure to corporal punishment is a risk factor for both immediate and long-term mental health problems, but along with exposure to corporal punishment there may be other risk factors or protective factors that increase or decrease the probability for mental health concerns in children who are exposed to physical discipline.

Several studies report parental factors as instrumental in predicting long-term corporal punishment related distress. Whether it is maternal anxiety and depression or an absent paternal figure (Bordin et al., 2009), general socioeconomic disadvantage (Sheu, Polcari, & Teicher, 2010), or lack of co-parental support (Lee, Guterman, & Lee, 2008), the current state of the parent can be a useful indicator of the child's mental health prognosis. Evidence suggests that common co-occuring issues such as parental substance abuse, parental mental illness, and adult domestic violence are associated with parenting behaviors that may escalate to child physical abuse and maltreatment (Barth, 2009).

In a large-scale, community study Lee, Perron, Taylor, and Guterman (2011) found that paternal education levels could have an impact on the severity of corporal punishment implemented on the child. Their findings showed that fathers who had completed high school (or educational equivalent) were more likely to utilize heavy corporal punishment than fathers who did not have a high school degree. Their study also found that while higher education status was an indicator of spanking, it was not an indicator of other corporal punishment practices.

In addition to the aforementioned predictors of risk, culture and ethnicity may link to the types of corporal punishment used as well as the psychological outcomes of the children who have been exposed to corporal punishment. In their community study, Lee et al. (2011) observed that, while African-American fathers were more likely than Caucasian-American fathers to engage in moderate corporal punishment, African-American fathers were no more likely to engage in heavy corporal punishment than Caucasian-American fathers. This illustrated that between different cultures the level of corporal punishment that the child experiences can vary, which could be a predictor of long-term wellbeing and mental health.

While culture can be an indicator of risk, some studies have found that culture and ethnicity may also be associated with certain protective factors for long-term well-being despite the occurrence of corporal punishment. Several studies have found a significant relationship between corporal punishment and behavioral issues with Caucasian-Americans, while also reporting a weak or non-significant relationship between corporal punishment and behavioral problems among African-Americans (Lansford, 2010). Another study of Cambodian, Chinese, Laotian or Mien and Vietnamese adolescents found no link between the respondents' reports of severe discipline, including corporal punishment, and reports of their own delinquency (Le, Monfared & Stockdale, 2005). These examples show that the overall effect of corporal punishment may not be universal. Additionally to this, other studies have indicated that exposure to corporal punishment in childhood may result in fewer long-term behavioral issues (Lansford, 2010).

It is also possible that context serves as the great equivocator in most cases. Because corporal punishment is only one part of the parent/child relationship, research has begun to indicate that familial support and positive parental relationships could serve as protective factors that might prevent negative outcomes from corporal punishment (Harper, Brown, Arias, & Brody 2006). Lansford (2010) also explored that parental warmth could counteract the negative effects of corporal punishment. She explains that the child's understanding of the punishment as a whole can serve as a tool to both reinforce positive behaviors as well as the parent/child relationship. If the child sees the punishment as reasonable and predictable, then they are less likely to experience distress. If corporal punishmentis part of a clear parenting plan then the child will know when it will occur as well as why it will occur, whereas if the corporal punishment is used as a result of parental anger or distress, the child will not be able to predict the response, resulting in a more fearful and anxiety-provoking dynamic. Lansford (2010) states that "if the children view the use of corporal punishment as "good" and caring parenting then there may be no relationship between the type of discipline and the child's adjustment later in life" (p. 98).

CONCLUSION

If corporal punishment is documented as causing pervasive negative outcomes throughout lifespan, then why doesn't the United States legislate against the practice as a whole? Gersoff (2010) believes the answer is twofold. Firstly, America has historically culturally embraced corporal punishment. The prevalence of corporal punishment in America remained high throughout the twentieth century (Hess et al., 2012), suggesting that many current parents who utilize corporal punishment experienced corporal punishment themselves. Gersoff (2010) notes, "As a result of this long history, corporal punishment has a strong intergenerational tradition in the United States." Secondly, Gersoff (2010) explained that Christianity influences parents to "make connections between firm discipline and a child's spiritual well-being, and encourage parents to use corporal punishment as an important part of their discipline repertoire." However, it is important to note that Jackson et al. (1999) previously found that "the less important religion was to parents, the more likely they were to have positive attitudes towards physical discipline."

Although there is much work to be done in terms of educating caregivers on best parenting practices it is encouraging to see that even without explicit legislation, the use of corporal punishment appears to be declining in America. Population surveys that rely on self reported data indicate that corporal punishment has dropped 18% over the last three decades (Zoltor, 2010). The Fourth National Incidence Study of Child Abuse and Neglect, a report presented to congress by Sedlak and colleagues in 2010, suggests a nationwide decline of 19% in the overall number of maltreated children in the United States since 2005-2006. In addition to this, the study also found a 26% decrease in the rate of overall harm and standard maltreatment per 1,000 children in the population.

Afifi et al. (2012) advise both parents and health care workers who treat children "to be aware of the link between physical punishment and mental disorders...[and] the adverse outcomes associated with exposure to physical punishment." Barth (2009) recommends increased public support for research trials to compare the effectiveness of programs focused on parenting education to enact more effective behavioral management methods, and those programs aiming to reduce related risk factors such as parental mental illness, parental substance abuse, and child behavioral problems. In a system already scrambling to find funding to adequately serve its patients, the government's continued inaction involving specific legislation against corporal punishment might lead to the proliferation of a practice that will exact an untenable physical, emotional, and monetary toll on its citizens.

REFERENCES

Afifi, T. O., Enns, M. W., Cox, B. J., Asmundson, G. J., Stein, M. B., & Sareen, J. (2008). Population attributable fractions of psychiatric disorders and suicide ideation and attempts associated with adverse childhood experiences. *Journal Information*, 98(5).

Afifi, T. O., Mota, N. P., Dasiewicz, P., MacMillan, H. L., & Sareen, J. (2012). Physical punishment and mental disorders: results from a nationally representative US sample. *Pediatrics*, 130(2), 184-192.

Appleton, J. V., & Stanley, N. (2011) Physical abuse and corporal punishment. *Child Abuse Review*, 21: 1-5.

Barth, R. P. (2009). Preventing child abuse and neglect with parent training: Evidence and opportunities. *The Future of Children*, 2, 95-118.

Berlin, L. J., Ispa, J. M., Fine, M. A., Malone, P. S., Brooks-Gunn, J., Brady-Smith, C., …Bai, Y. (2010) Correlates and consequences of spanking and verbal punishment for low-income White, African American, and Mexican American toddlers. *Child Development*.;80:1403–1420.

Bordin, I. A., Duarte, C. S., Peres, C. A., Nascimento, R., Curto, B. M., & Paula, C. S. (2009). Severe physical punishment: risk of mental health problems for poor urban children in Brazil. *Bulletin of the World Health Organization*, 87(5), 336-344.

Boutwell, B. B., Franklin, C. A., Barnes, J. C., & Beaver, K. M. (2011). Physical punishment and childhood aggression: the role of gender and gene–environment interplay. *Aggressive behavior*, 37(6), 559-568.

Callender, K. A., Olson, S. L., Choe, D. E., & Sameroff, A. J. (2012). The effects of parental depressive symptoms, appraisals, and physical punishment on later child externalizing behavior. *Journal of abnormal child psychology*, 40(3), 471-483.

Cheng, H. G., Anthony, J. C., & Huang, Y. (2010). Harsh physical punishment as a specific childhood adversity linked to adult drinking consequences: evidence from China. *Addiction*, 105(12), 2097-2105.

Eyberg, S. M. (2004). The PCIT story part 1: Conceptual foundation. PCIT Pages: The *Parent-Child Interaction Therapy Newsletter*, 1, 1-2.

Eyberg, S. M. (2005). Tailoring and adapting parent-child interaction therapy for new population. *Education and Treatment of Children*, 28, 197-201.

Fatori, D., Bordin, I. A., Curto, B. M., de Paula, C. S., (2013) Influence of psychosicial risk factors on the trajectory of mental health problems from childhood to adolescence: a longitudinal study. *BMC Psychiatry*, 13:31.

Gershoff, E. T., (2010) More harm than good: a summary of scientific research on the intended and unintended effects of corporal punishment on children. *Law and Contemporary Problems.* 73:31.

Harper, F. W. K., Brown, A. M., Arias, I., & Brody, G. (2006). Corporal punishment and kids: How do parent support and gender influence child adjustment? Journal of Family Violence, 21(3), 197–207.

Hess, C. A., Gray, J. M., Nunez, N. L. (2012) The effect of social dominance orientation on perceptions of corporal punishment *Journal of Interpersonal Violence* 27: 2728.

Kvam, M. H., & Loeb, M. (2010). The relation between adverse childhood experiences and later mental health among deaf adults. *Scandinavian Journal of Disability Research*, 12(4), 233-244.

Lansford, J. E. (2010). The special problem of cultural differences in effects of corporal punishment. Law and Contemporary Problems, 73, 89–106.

Lansford, J. E., Criss, M. M., Laird, R. D., Shaw, D. S., Pettit, G. S., Bates, J. E., & Dodge, K. A. (2011). Reciprocal relations between parents' physical discipline and children's externalizing behavior during middle childhood and adolescence. *Development and psychopathology*, 23(01), 225-238.

Le, T. N., Monfared, G., & Stockdale, G. D. (2005). The Relationship of School, Parent, and Peer Contextual Factors with Self-Reported Delinquency for Chinese, Cambodian, Laotian or Mien, and Vietnamese Youth. *Crime & Delinquency*, 51(2), 192-219.

Lee, S. J., Guterman, N. B., & Lee, Y. (2008). Risk factors for paternal physical child abuse. *Child Abuse & Neglect,* 32, 846-858.

Lee, S. J., Perron, B. E., Taylor, C. A., & Guterman, N. B. (2011). Paternal psychosocial characteristics and corporal punishment of their 3-year-old children. *Journal of interpersonal violence*, 26(1), 71-87.

Lenta, P. (2012). Corporal Punishment of Children. *Social Theory and Practice*, 38(4), 689-716.

Lundahl, B. W., Nimer, J., & Parsons, B. (2006). Preventing child abuse: A meta-analysis of parent training programs. Research on Social Work Practice, 16, 251-262.

Ma, J., Han, Y., Grogan-Kaylor, A., Delva, J., & Castillo, M. (2012). Corporal punishment and youth externalizing behavior in Santiago, Chile. *Child abuse & neglect.* 36, 481-490.

MacMillan, H. L., Boyle, M. H., Wong, M. Y. Y., Duku, E. K., Fleming, J. E., & Walsh, C. A. (1999). Slapping and spanking in childhood and its association with lifetime prevalence of psychiatric disorders in a general population sample. *Canadian Medical Association Journal*, 161(7), 805-809.

Nowak, C. & Heinrichs, N. (2008). A comprehensive meta-analysis of Triple P - Positive Parenting Program using hierarchical linear modeling: Effectiveness and moderating variables. *Clinical Child and Family Psychology Review*, 11, 114-144.

Oates, K. (2011). Physical punishment of children: Can we continue to accept the status quo? *Journal of Paediatrics and Child Health*, 47(8), 505-507.

Pearl, E. S. (2008). Parent-Child Interaction Therapy with an immigrant family exposed to domestic violence. *Clinical Case Studies*, 7, 25-41.

Sanapo, M. S., & Nakamura, Y. (2011). Gender and physical punishment: the filipino children's experience. *Child Abuse Review*, 20(1), 39-56.

Sedlak, A. J., Mettenburg, J., Basena, M., Peta, I., McPherson, K., & Greene, A. (2010). Fourth national incidence study of child abuse and neglect (NIS-4). *Washington, DC: US Department of Health and Human Services.*

Sheu, Y. S., Polcari, A., Anderson, C. M., & Teicher, M. H. (2010). Harsh corporal punishment is associated with increased T2 relaxation time in dopamine-rich regions. *Neuroimage*, 53(2), 412-419.

Taylor, C. A., Mangarella, J. A., Lee, S. J., Rice, J. C. (2010) Mothers' spanking of three-year-old children and subsequent risk of childrens' aggressive behavior. *Pediatrics*; 125: 1057–65.

Turner, H. A., & Muller, P. A. (2004). Long-term effects of child corporal punishment on depressive symptoms in young adults. *Journal of Family Issues*, 25, 761–782.

UNICEF(1989). Convention on the Rights of the Child. UNICEF: Geneva, Switzerland.

UNICEF (2006). Convention on the Rights of the Child: General Comment No. 8. UNICEF: Geneva, Switzerland.

Urquiza, A. J., & McNeil, C. B. (1996). Parent-child interaction therapy: An intensive dyadic intervention for physically abusive families. *Child Maltreatment,* 1, 134-144.

Webster-Stratton, C., & Taylor, T. (2001). Nipping early risk factors in the bud: Preventing substance abuse, delinquency, and violence in adolescence through interventions targeted at young children (0-8 years). *Prevention Science,* 2, 165-192.

Zolotor, A. J., Theodore, A. D., Runyan, D. K., Chang, J. J., & Laskey, A. L. (2011). Corporal punishment and physical abuse: population-based trends for three-to-11-year-old children in the United States. *Child Abuse Review*, 20(1), 57-66.

In: Psychology of Punishment
Editor: Nicolas Castro

ISBN: 978-1-62948-103-6
© 2013 Nova Science Publishers, Inc.

Chapter 6

THE ROLE OF GENDER AND SCHOOL TYPE IN EFL TEACHERS' ADOPTION OF CLASSROOM DISCIPLINE STRATEGIES

Mehrak Rahimi and Fatemeh Hosseini Karkami*
[1]English Department, Faculty of Humanities,
Shahid Rajaee Teacher Training University, Lavizan, Tehran, Iran
[2]Mazandaran Office of Education, Sari, Iran

ABSTRACT

The aim of the current study was investigating the role of gender and school type (private and public) in EFL teachers' adoption of discipline strategies from their students' perspective. One thousand and four hundred eight students expressed their perceptions of the strategies their English teachers used to discipline the class on five main factors including punishment, recognition/reward, discussion, involvement/hinting, and aggression. The findings revealed that male and female teachers' adoption of discipline strategies was significantly different and female teachers were perceived to use punitive (punishment and aggression) and discussion strategies more frequently than male teachers. Further, it was found that public and private school teachers were different with respect to the strategies they implemented to discipline their classes. While public school teachers used aggression

---

* Email: mehrakrahimi@yahoo.com.

strategies more than private school teachers, private school teachers used discussion strategies more than public school teachers. The interaction of gender by school-type was also found to be statistically significant, implying that female teachers who worked in private schools tended to use involvement/hinting strategies more than other teachers while female teachers who worked in public schools were found to use punitive strategies more frequently in comparison to other teachers.

Keywords: Discipline; strategies; gender; school type; EFL

1. INTRODUCTION

Teachers are identified as a key factor in making learning effective and students' learning attitude and learning motivation are influenced both by their perceptions of what their teachers do in the classroom and directly by teachers' actual behavior (Allen, Witt, & Wheeless, 2006).

Factors such as teachers' personal characteristics, their teaching style, the strategies they use in the classroom, and the way they support and care for their students all combine to determine how teachers can motivate or demotivate their students. Classroom discipline is one of the most significant activities that shape a teacher's professional identity. In a supportive classroom climate where a teacher builds up good rapport with students and creates an atmosphere of warmth, safety, and acceptance, students become more self-initiated, self-confident, and self-directed learners (Brown, 2001). One way to create this atmosphere is to manage the class appropriately (Lewis, 2001). When teachers act offensively and punish students for minor forms of misbehavior, learning is negatively affected and students report more psychological and somatic complaints (Sava, 2002).

Classroom management particularly raises key issues in EFL classes as maintaining discipline in a class that needs lots of group or pair work is challenging for many teachers (Linse & Nunan, 2005). On the one hand, a language teacher should prepare the ground for communicative activities by lowering students' inhibition, anxiety, and fear (Richards & Rogers, 2003). On the other hand, to help students benefit from instruction, the teacher should maintain order in the classroom. This creates confusion among many language teachers and may lead to adoption of contradictory management strategies that ultimately affects students' attitudes and learning (Ormrod, 2003, Cited in Kang, 2013).

1.1. Classroom Discipline Strategies

While discipline to the laymen and even some experts is associated with punishment and control, it does not always demand a series of punishments applied to manage misbehaving students. For many educationists disciplining a classroom equals a kind of contract which connects a teacher and a group of students to effectively manage the classroom so that learning can be more efficient (Harmer, 1983).

There are at least three main approaches to classroom discipline, each advocating particular techniques. Some educationalists argue that in order to promote responsibility in children, teachers need to clarify their expectations of student behavior and then sensibly use a range of rewards for good behavior as well as punishment for misbehavior (Canter & Canter, 2002). Others argue that disciplining a classroom can only be attained by investing more on student self-regulation through using techniques such as negotiating, discussing, and contracting rather than student obedience and teacher coercion (Vitto, 2003). The third orientation favors group participation and decision making, based on which the group takes responsibility for ensuring the appropriateness of the behavior of all its members (Edwards & Mullis, 2003). The importance of classroom discipline lies in the fact that it can lead to developing an effective classroom management style which may guarantee higher academic performance among students, help them focus on doing educational tasks by developing a sense of responsibility, and minimize chaos and disruptive behavior when teaching is in progress (Lewis, Romi, Katz, & Qui, 2008).

Some educationists consider classroom discipline and classroom management as being synonymous (e.g., Ellis & Karr-Kidwell, 1995; Kohn, 1994; Tauber, 1995). However, there are a considerable number of experts (e.g., Martin, Yin & Baldwin, 1997; McLaughlin, 1994; Ralph, 1994) who differentiate between classroom management and classroom discipline. In this respect, Lewis (1997) asserts that "discipline can be distinguished from the broader area of classroom management" (p. 404), as classroom management means managing instruction, organizing materials and learning activities and aims at decreasing the rate of off-task behaviors; while discipline embodies the strategies teachers implement after misbehaviors occur (Lewis, 1997).

Recent research on classroom discipline suggests that teachers widely use a number of discipline strategies to control disruptions in their classes as the number of misbehaving students has increased lately (Lewis, 2001). Some of them, such as punitive strategies have been found to be of limited usefulness in promoting responsible student behavior as the degree of misbehavior severity may increase as the teacher imposes more punishment (Lewis, 2001). Thus the class is put in a vicious cycle of aggression and punishment. In contrast, as literature shows, there are some discipline strategies that are more productive and valuable in promoting students' responsibility and decreasing the reoccurrence of misbehavior. These may include recognition of students' responsible behavior by the teacher or having discussion with those who misbehave about the impact their behavior has on others (Lewis, et al., 2008).

1.2. Classroom Discipline and Language Classes

In English classes adoption of appropriate discipline strategies plays a key role in both teaching and learning. As the goal of English classes is the development of communicative competence, students should experience activities that require active participation and collaboration in groups or pairs. As a result of that "students usually have more opportunities in an EFL class than classes of other subjects to speak, to talk, to read loud or even to argue with each other" (Yi, 2006, p. 132).

These types of classes thus demand careful management from the teacher's side, because if inappropriate discipline strategies that do not match communicative activities are implemented in language classes, communicative approaches will have little impact on students' interest to learn a foreign language (Tomlinson, 1988).

Wadden and McGovern (1991) list the following factors that affect disciplining a language class: large number of students who are not in the classroom by choice; number of students per class; the lack of importance students give to English in the school curriculum in comparison to other school subjects; and students' cultural and academic backgrounds. Brown (2007) underscores the importance of discipline in language classes by saying that, "if all of your students were hardworking, intrinsically motivated, active, dedicated intelligent learners - well, you would still have what we could label as discipline problems!" (p. 417).

Despite recent advances in research and theorization in teachers' discipline strategies, there is a dearth of research to investigate EFL teachers' discipline strategies and the effect of teacher' gender and context of teaching on their strategy use and preference. The current study thus answers the following questions:

(1) Does gender have a role in EFL teachers' adoption of discipline strategies?

(2) Does teaching context have a role in EFL teachers' adoption of discipline strategies?

2. METHOD

2.1. Participants

The population of the study included all grade one and two junior high-school students in an urban area in Iran. The sample was selected based on cluster random sampling from 35 private and public schools of district 1 of the city that included 19 girls' schools (12 public, 7 private) and 16 boys' schools (10 public, and 6 private).

Based on Krejcie and Morgan's (1970) formula with confidence level of 95% (margin of error = 2.5%) the sample size was determined to be 1275. To select the sample, the list of schools was taken from the educational office and 26 schools were randomly selected to be included in the study.

From each school 2 classes (one grade 1 and one grade 2) were selected randomly and participated in the study (52 classes, altogether). Of the sample 628 (44%) were female and 1061 students (75%) were studying in public schools.

It should be noted that the gender of teachers and students were the same in all schools, i.e., girls had female teachers and boys had male teachers.

2.2. The Instrument

2.2.1. Classroom Discipline Strategies Questionnaire

To measure teachers' classroom discipline strategies, the 24-item questionnaire of classroom discipline (Lewis, 2001) was used. The scale measures six discipline strategies including punishment, recognition/reward, discussion, involvement, hinting, and aggression.

In order to assess teachers' discipline strategies, students were asked to indicate 'how frequently the teacher acted as described in the statement when trying to deal with misbehavior' on a 6-point Likert type scale.

The response alternatives provided were Nearly always (6), Most of the time (5), A lot of the time (4), Some of the time (3), Hardly ever (2) and Never (1).

Validation of the Persian version of the questionnaire has shown that the questionnaire items load on 5 factors (Rahimi & Hosseini, 2011). As hinting and involvement strategies load on the same factor, they were considered one type of strategy in this study.

The Cronbach's alpha reliability of the scale was found to be .81. The following reliability coefficients were estimated for five factors of the questionnaire: .79 for punishment; .73 for rewarding/recognition; .74 for involvement/hinting; .75 for aggression; and .81 for discussion.

2.2.2. A Personal Information Form

A personal information form was used to gather data about the participants' demographic information such as age, gender, school type, and grade.

3. RESULTS

3.1. Descriptive Statistics

Table 1 summarizes means and standard deviations of classroom discipline strategies by gender and school type.

As Table 1 shows, the average score of discipline strategies is 3.40, while each item was measured by a 6-point likert scale, implying that EFL teachers frequently use classroom discipline strategies to manage their classes. Further, they prefer to use recognition/reward strategies (mean=4.29) most of the time while they tend to avoid aggression (mean=2.48) and punishment (mean=2.72) strategies in their classes.

Examining the means of male and female teachers shows that female teachers on average use discipline strategies (mean=3.56) more than male teachers do (mean=3.27). They also use punishment, aggression, and discussion strategies more in comparison to male teachers.

Examining the means of private and public school teachers shows that on average public school teachers use discipline strategies (mean=3.43) more than private school teachers do (mean=3.31). They also use punishment, aggression, and discussion strategies more than private school teachers do.

Table 1. Descriptive statistics of classroom discipline strategies by gender and school type

Variables	Male (n=780)		Female (n=628)		Public (n=1061)		Private (n=347)		Total sample (n=1408)	
	Mean	SD	Mean	SD	Mean	SD	Mean	SD	Mean	SD
Classroom discipline	3.27	.725	3.56	.746	3.43	.758	3.31	.714	3.40	.748
Involvement/hinting	3.84	1.16	3.81	1.10	3.84	1.27	3.78	1.17	3.83	1.40
Punishment	2.30	1.11	3.23	1.24	2.76	1.28	2.59	1.16	2.72	1.25
Recognition/reward	4.35	1.40	4.22	1.41	4.29	1.39	4.31	1.49	4.29	1.41
Aggression	2.15	1.27	2.90	1.40	2.53	1.38	2.34	1.37	2.48	1.38
Discussion	2.89	1.19	3.42	1.22	3.11	1.20	2.83	1.23	3.04	1.22

3.2. Gender, School Type, and Classroom Discipline Strategies

In order to investigate the differences between EFL teachers' discipline strategies considering gender and school type, a 2-way MANOVA was conducted in which the five classroom discipline strategies served as the dependent variables and gender (2 levels) and school type (2 levels, private and public) acted as two independent variables.

The results from the Multivariate tests for the first main effect suggested that there was a statistically significant difference between male and female teachers on the combined dependent variables (Wilks' Lambda=.909, F=27.926, p=.000, partial eta squared=.091).

As Table 2 shows, when the results for the dependent variables were considered separately, the differences to reach the statistical significance, using a Bonferroni adjusted alpha level of .025 (Tabachnick & Fidell, 2007), were punishment (F=131.416, p=.000), aggression (F=37.545, p=.000), and discussion (F=22.230, p=.000). Comparing the mean differences showed that female teachers were perceived to use aggression, punishment, and discussion strategies more than their male counterparts (Table 1).

Investigating the second main effect showed that there was a statistically significant difference between private and public school teachers on the combined dependent variables (Wilks' Lambda=.987, F=3.662, p=.033, partial eta squared=.013).

As Table 3 shows, when the results for the dependent variables were considered separately, the only differences to reach the statistical significance were aggression (F=8.00, p=.005) and discussion (F=11.621, p=.001). Comparing means showed that public school teachers were perceived to use aggression strategies more than private school teachers while private school teachers were perceived to use discussion strategies more than public school teachers (Table 1).

Table 2. Tests of Between-Subjects Effects for the first main effect (gender)

Source	Dependent Variable	Sum of Squares	Mean Square	F	p	Partial Eta Squared
Gender	Punishment	176.882	176.882	131.416	.000	.086
	Aggression	64.944	64.944	37.545	.000	.026
	Discussion	32.338	32.338	22.230	.000	.016

Table 3. Tests of Between-Subjects Effects for the second main effect (school type)

Source	Dependent Variable	Sum of Squares	Mean Square	F	p	Partial Eta Squared
School	Aggression	13.841	13.841	8.00	.005	.006
type	Discussion	16.905	16.905	11.621	.001	.008

Table 4. Tests of Between-Subjects Effects for the interaction effect (gender by school type)

Source	Dependent Variable	Sum of Squares	Mean Square	F	p	Partial Eta Squared
Interaction of gender by school	Involvement /hinting	8.597	8.597	6.632	.010	.005
type	Punishment	11.287	11.287	8.386	.004	.006
	Aggression	65.427	65.427	37.824	.000	.026

The interaction of gender by school type was also found to be statistically significant (Wilks' Lambda=.960, F=11.645, p=.000, partial eta squared=.040).

As Table 4 shows, when the results for the dependent variables were considered separately, the differences to reach the statistical significance were involvement/hinting (F=6.632, p=.010), punishment (F=8.386, p=.004), and aggression (F=37.824, p=.000).

Comparing the means showed that female teachers who worked in private schools tended to use involvement/hinting strategies more than other teachers (mean=3.91). On the other hand, female teachers who worked in public schools were found to use punishment (mean=3.31) and aggression (mean=3.07) strategies more than other teachers.

4. DISCUSSION

The aim of the current study was to find the role of gender and teaching context in EFL teachers' adoption of discipline strategies to manage students' misbehavior in their classes.

The findings revealed that female EFL teachers were more authoritarian than male teachers and used aggression and punishment strategies more frequently. There are mixed findings with respect to the way male and female teachers manage their classes (e.g., Martin & Yin, 1997). However, a few studies support the fact that female teachers resort to coercive strategies to reorient misbehavior (Lewis, Romi, Xing, & Katz, 2005) because female teachers perceive behavior challenges to be more severe than do their male colleagues (Green, Shriberg, & Farber, 2008).

In spite of the fact that female teachers were perceived to be more authoritarian teachers, their use of discussion strategies in the classroom was found to be more than male teachers. In other words, they used discipline strategies that help them to organize the class to work out the rules for good behavior, decide with the class what should happen to students who misbehave (most probably punishing them), and let students know that the way they are behaving is not how the class expects them to (Lewis, et al. 2005). While this finding at first glance seems to be contradictory with their adoption of punitive strategies, it is not if one considers postulations with respect to gendered nature of teaching in which female teachers' behavior is linked to nurturance and caring behavior of mothers (Burgess & Carter, 1992). Similarities between teachers and mothers' role have been discussed and it is generally believed that female "teachers are invariably and ultimately (at the very core of their being) mothers" (Lightfoot, 1978, p. 69). Thus, like being in a mother-child relationship, teachers are continuously involved in establishing caring relations with students by adapting both mothering and disciplining strategies.

It was also found that the context of teaching influences the use of certain strategies as public school EFL teachers were found to use aggression strategies more than private school teachers while private school teachers were perceived to use discussion strategies more than public school teachers. Teaching behavior cannot be easily understood when the original context of the specific teaching behavior is not included in the interpretation (Lowyck, 1987, Cited in Korthagen, 2004). School facilities, administrative support, class size, salary, work load, respect and recognition, commute time, resources for students, students' socioeconomic status, student ethnicity, and student performance are among the components of work environment that can affect teachers' behavior (Horng, 2009; Malakolunthu, Idris, & Rengasamy, 2010), professional knowledge/competencies (ten Dam & Blom, 2006), and beliefs (Isikoglu, Basturk, & Karaca, 2009).

Evidence shows that one of the non-academic advantages private schools offer over public schools is more discipline and security (Martínez-Mora, 2006). The administrative policy is to manage the school in a way that limited instances of misbehavior happen in school in general and in classes in particular to increase student ability and school quality (Cherchye, Witte,

Ooghe, & Nicaise, 2010). Thus, students in private schools are more polite and show less disruptive behavior (Rabiei & Salehi, 2007). Consequently less coercive behaviors are shown by teachers who work in private schools. Further, teachers who work in private schools have higher job satisfaction (Papanastasiou & Zembylas, 2005) and commitment (Tooley & Dixon, 2007) and hold more learner-centered beliefs (Razmjou, 2006). Thus they may spend more time on interacting with students and discussing misbehavior-if that happens- with students in comparison to public school teachers.

The interaction effect of gender and context of teaching was also found to be influential on teachers' adoption of classroom discipline strategies. This can be discussed from two perspectives. First punishment and aggression strategies were found to be used most frequently by female teachers who worked in public schools. As girls' public schools were found to be more populated in this study, female teachers' aggressive behavior can be attributed to the number of students in each class (Brown, 2001) that results in negative participation and misbehavior.

Second, it was found that female teachers who worked in private schools tended to involve their students in classroom discipline decisions and were supportive of students' voices in this regard more than other teachers. As the hallmark of femininity is relationality, responsive, caring, and empathetic connection with others (Gilligan, 1993), based on this finding, if the ground is ready for female teachers (in terms of working condition) they will show their full-fledged teacher-mother character that is associated with fostering growth and change, acceptability, and attentive love (Abbey, 2000, Cited in Pflum, 2005). In this way they connect teaching with mothering through images of caring and nurturance (Goldstein & Lake, 2000).

REFERENCES

Allen, M., Witt, P.L., & Wheeless, L. R. (2006). The role of teacher immediacy as a motivational factor in student learning: Using meta-analysis to test a causal model. *Communication Education, 55,* 21-31.

Brown, H. D. (2007). *Principles of language learning and teaching* (5th Ed.). Englewood Cliffs, NJ: Prentice Hall Regents.

Brown, H. D. (2001). *Teaching by principles.* White Plains, NY: Pearson Education LTD.

Burgess, H., & Carter, B. (1992). Bringing out the best in people: Teacher training and the 'real' teacher. *British Journal of Sociology of Education, 13*, 349-359.

Canter, L., & Canter, M. (2002). *Lee Canter's assertive discipline.* Santa Monica, CA: Lee Canter & Associates.

Cherchye, L., Witte, K.D., Ooghe, E., & Nicaise, I. (2010). Efficiency and Equity in private and public education: A nonparametric comparison. *European Journal of Operational Research, 202*, 563-573.

Edwards, D., & Mullis, F. (2003). Classroom meetings: Encouraging a climate of cooperation. *Professional School Counseling, 7*, 20-27.

Ellis, D. W., & Karr-Kidwell, P. J. (1995). A study of assertive discipline and recommendations for effective classroom management methods. (Eric Document Reproduction Service No. ED 379 207).

Gilligan, C. (1993). *In a different voice.* Cambridge, MA: Harvard University Press.

Goldstein, L., & Lake, V. (2000). Love, love, and more love for children. Exploring pre-service teachers' understandings of caring. *Teaching and Teacher Education, 16*, 861-872.

Green, S.P., Shriberg, D., & Farber, S. (2008). What's gender got to do with it? Teachers' perceptions of situation severity and requests for assistance. *Journal for Educational and Psychological Consultation, 18*, 346-373.

Harmer, J. (1983). *The practice of English language teaching.* London: Longman.

Horng, E. L. (2009). Teacher tradeoffs: Disentangling teachers' preferences for working conditions and student demographics. *American Educational Research Journal, 46*, 690-717.

Isikoglu, N., Basturk, R., and Karaca, F. (2009). Assessing in-service teachers' instructional beliefs about student-centered education: A Turkish perspective. *Teaching and Teacher Education, 25*, 350-356.

Kang, D. M. (2013). EFL teachers' language use for classroom discipline: A look at complex interplay of variables. *System, 41, 149-163.*

Kohn, A. (1994). Bribes for behaving: Why Behaviorism doesn't help children become good people. *The NAMTA Journal, 19*, 71-94.

Korthagen, F. A. J. (2004). In search of the essence of a good teacher: Towards a more holistic approach in teacher education. *Teaching and Teacher Education, 20, 77-97.*

Krejcie, R., & Morgan, D. (1970). Determining sample size for research activities. *Educational and Psychological Measurement, 30*, 607-610.

Lewis, R., (1997). *The discipline dilemma* (2nd ed.). Melbourne: The Australian Council for Educational Research.

Lewis, R. (2001). Classroom discipline and student responsibility: The students' view. *Teaching and Teacher Education, 17*, 307-319.

Lewis, R., Romi, S., Xing, Q., & Katz, Y. (2005). A comparison of teachers' classroom discipline in Australia, China and Israel. *Teaching and Teacher Education, 21,* 729-741.

Lewis, R., Romi, S., Katz, Y. J., & Qui, X. (2008). Students' reaction to classroom discipline in Australia, Israel, and China. *Teaching and Teacher Education, 24,* 715-724.

Lightfoot, S.L. (1978). *Worlds apart.* New York: Basic Books.

Linse, C., & Nunan, D. (2005). *Practical English language teaching.* US: McGraw-Hill.

Malakolunthu, S., Idris, A. R., & Rengasamy, N.C. (2010). Teacher professional experience and performance: Impact of the work environment and general welfare in Malaysian secondary schools. *Asia Pacific Education Review, 11,* 609-617.

Martin, N., & Yin, Z. (1997). *Attitudes and beliefs regarding classroom management style: Differences between male and female teachers.* Paper presented at the annual meeting of the Southwest Educational Research Association, Austin, TX. (ERIC Document Reproduction Service No. ED 404738).

Martin, N. K., Yin, Z., & Baldwin, B. (1997). Classroom management training, class size and graduate study: Do these variables impact teachers' beliefs regarding classroom management style? (Eric Document Reproduction Service No. ED 420 671).

Martinez-Mora, F. (2006). The existence of non-elite private schools. *Journal of Public Economics, 90,* 1505-1518.

McLaughlin, H. J. (1994). From negation to negotiation: Moving away from the management metaphor. *Action in Teacher Education, XVI,* 75-84.

Papanastasiou, E. C., & Zembylas, M. (2005). Job satisfaction variance among public and private kindergarten school teachers in Cyprus. *International Journal of Educational Research, 43,* 147-167.

Pflum, L. M. (2005). *Mother teachers living on the edges: Idealized conceptions and miserable realities.* Doctoral Dissertation. US: The University of Texas.

Rabiei, M., & Salehi, R. (2007). Comparison between training ratios and quality of education in the best private and governmental schools in the province of Chaharmahal and Bakhtiari in Iran. *Journal of Educational Innovations, 6*, 109-140. Available online: www.sid.ir.

Rahimi, M. & Hosseini, M. (2011). *The role of EFL teachers' classroom discipline strategies in their professional success and students' language learning motivation.* Unpublished MA thesis. Iran: Shahid Rajaee Teacher Training. Available online: www.irandoc.ac.ir

Rahimi, M., & Asadollahi, F. (2012). EFL teachers' classroom management orientations: Investigating the role of individual differences and contextual variables. *Procedia Social and Behavioral Sciences, 31*, 43-48.

Ralph, E.G. (1994). Middle and secondary L2 teachers meeting classroom management challenges via effective teaching research. *Foreign Language Annals, 27*, 89-103.

Razmjou, S.A. (2006). *On the practicality of communicative language teaching in two domains of an expanding circle: Local public and private EFL institutes.* Unpublished MA thesis. Iran: Shiraz University. Available online www.irandoc.ir.

Richards, J. C., & Rogers, T. (2003). *Approaches and methods and in language teaching.* Cambridge: Cambridge University Press.

Sava, F. A. (2002). Causes and effects of teacher conflict-inducing attitudes towards pupils: A path analysis model. *Teaching and Teacher Education, 18*, 1007-1027.

Tabachnik, B. G., & Fidell, L. S. (2007). *Using multivariate statistics* (5th ed.). Boston: Pearson Education.

Tauber, R. T. (1995). *Classroom management: Theory and practice* (2nd ed.). NY: Harcourt, Brace.

ten Dam, G., & Blom, S. (2006). Learning through participation. The potential of school based teacher education for developing a professional identity. *Teaching and Teacher Education, 22*, 647-660.

Tomlinson, B. (1988). Conflicts in TEFL: Reasons for failure in secondary schools. *Institute of Language in Education Journal, 4*, 103-110.

Tooley, J., & Dixon, P. (2007). Private schooling for low-income families: A census and comparative survey in East Delhi, India. *International Journal of Educational Development, 27*, 205-219.

Vitto, J. M. (2003). *Relationship-driven classroom management: Strategies that promote student motivation.* Thousand Oaks, CA: Corwin Press.

Wadden, P., & McGovern, S. (1991). The quandary of negative class participation: Coming to terms with misbehavior in the language classroom. *ELT Journal, 45*, 119-127.

Williams, M., & Burden, R. (1997). *Psychology for language teachers.* Cambridge: Cambridge University Press.

Yi, F. (2006). EFL classroom management: Creating a positive climate for learning. Retrieved January 2012 from wlkc.nbu.edu.cn/jpkc_nbu/ daxueyingyu/download/013.pdf

INDEX

S

T

U

V

W

Y